"The book addresses human vulnerabilities such as facing failure and lacking validation and love. Melissa has not only overcome these vulnerabilities but is also one of the best-qualified people to lead you through the tunnel of failure to the light at the end – SUCCESS!"

–Joseph Luckett,
 International Best Selling Author

"This book captivates and engages the reader to explore key breakthrough methods of claiming your comeback regardless of status, upbringing, or hardship. Every chapter was refreshing, authentic, and cultivating."

–Pastor Dunamis Duplessis,
 Founder of The Preachers League

CLAIM YOUR COMEBACK

Begin Your Journey to Healing and Wholeness

by Melissa Jones

Living Healed Publishing

Claim Your Comeback

Begin Your Journey to Healing and Wholeness
Melissa Jones
Living Healed Publishing

Published by Living Healed Publishing, O'Fallon, MO
Copyright ©2022 Melissa Jones
All rights reserved.

No part of this publication may be reproduced, stored in a retrieval system, or transmitted in any form or by any means, electronic, mechanical, photocopying, recording, scanning, or otherwise, except as permitted under Section 107 or 108 of the 1976 United States Copyright Act, without the prior written permission of the Publisher. Requests to the Publisher for permission should be addressed to Permissions Department, Living Healed Publishing, melissa@livinghealedministries.com.

Limit of Liability/Disclaimer of Warranty: While the publisher and author have used their best efforts in preparing this book, they make no representations or warranties with respect to the accuracy or completeness of the contents of this book and specifically disclaim any implied warranties of merchantability or fitness for a particular purpose. No warranty may be created or extended by sales representatives or written sales materials. The advice and strategies contained herein may not be suitable for your situation. You should consult with a professional where appropriate. Neither the publisher nor author shall be liable for any loss of profit or any other commercial damages, including but not limited to special, incidental, consequential, or other damages.

Cover Design: K Sonderegger / MadeYouLook.net

Editor: Anya Overmann / AnyaOvermann.com

Project Management and Interior design:
Davis Creative, CreativePublishingPartners.com

Library of Congress Cataloging-in-Publication Data

Library of Congress Control Number: 2022905660

Melissa Jones

Claim Your Comeback: Begin Your Journey to Healing and Wholeness

ISBN: 979-8-9859284-0-2 (Paperback)
      979-8-9859284-2-6 (Hardback)
      979-8-9859284-1-9 (ebook)

BISAC Subject headings:

1.) SEL000000   SELF-HELP / General   2. FAM001000   FAMILY & RELATIONSHIPS / Abuse / General   3. FAM001030   FAMILY & RELATIONSHIPS / Abuse / Domestic Partner Abuse

2022

ATTENTION CORPORATIONS, UNIVERSITIES, COLLEGES AND PROFESSIONAL ORGANIZATIONS: Quantity discounts are available on bulk purchases of this book for educational, gift purposes, or as premiums for increasing magazine subscriptions or renewals. Special books or book excerpts can also be created to fit specific needs. For information, please contact Living Healed Publishing, melissa@livinghealedministries.com.

DEDICATION

I want to dedicate this book to my deceased paternal grandmother Vashtye Buckels, or "Tye," as she was lovingly known. She was the strongest woman I've known on this earth. She raised 12 children as a single mother and did so with a robustness that only came from God. After she and my grandfather divorced, he moved to California and started a new life. She managed to raise my father and his siblings on her own while working two jobs. She was incredibly independent, living alone until she passed away at 84.

When I was going through my divorce, she came to the divorce hearings to support me. "If I did it with 12 kids, you can do it with three," she would say. Her powerful words kept me going. I ended up becoming depressed, and through my bouts of depression, my aunt would remind me, "you've got Tye's blood in you." Her strength has been my inspiration through all of my challenges in life.

Thanks to my father, who has always been my cheerleader (and will hate this term because he's ex-military). He has supported me in every season of my life — including when I was not so loving. When I was off the chain acting outlandish, he continued to be my #1 supporter. He knows how to hold me accountable and call me out on the carpet in a way that I know he always has my back. He's just that type of father.

Love you, Dad.

To my mother, thank you for being there for my kids and me during the seasons after my divorce.

Left to Right: Me, oldest daughter Abriana, son Ajay, & youngest daughter Ari. Not pictured: Z.

I also want to dedicate this book to my children—Bri, Ajay, Ari, and my bonus son, Z. Like my Grandma Tye, I was a single working mother. When I first divorced, my kids provided the motivation I needed to keep going. I left home at 6 AM every weekday to drop them off at daycare before heading to work. Even though it was hard, even though there were many days that I didn't feel like it, I kept getting up and doing what I needed to do. I wanted to do it for them.

> Bri, Ajay, Ari, and my bonus son, Z:
> You are my pride and joy.
> I am so grateful God gave me each one of you.
> You have definitely been my greatest gift.
> Thank you for inspiring me to keep going.
> I love you to life.

ACKNOWLEDGMENTS

To all of my family and friends that walked this journey of healing with me, you were instrumental in helping me stay on the path to claim my comeback. I wholeheartedly thank you! I know dealing with me at certain times of my healing journey was not easy. You had a big assignment before you, and I appreciate everyone for loving me through it and walking it out with me. Even in seasons when I wanted to quit, you stayed, you prayed, and never gave up on me. Thank you for supporting me. I love each one of you to life.

And I'd like to thank everyone who worked with me on this project.

To Anya Overmann, who helped put my manuscript together, thank you for being patient with this technologically-challenged Gen Xer.

Thank you to K Sonderegger, who took my vision and made it a book cover.

Thank you to Cathy Davis and her publishing team for making publishing this book a reality.

Thank you to Rebecca Hall Gruyter and her marketing team for helping me get the exposure to make this book a success.

And to Joseph Luckett, the mastermind of networking and author of Zero to 100: The Gold Standard of Global Networking, who introduced me to all these people and helped me form this incredible team – thank you. We go back like Cadillacs!

I love you all, and I wouldn't be here without you.

CONTENTS

Foreword...xiii

Preface.. xv

Introduction: Claiming My Own Comeback.....................1

Chapter 1: Faith, Hope, & Your Vision.......................17

Chapter 2: Accepting Your Reality...........................29

Chapter 3: Identifying Roadblocks & Triggers 39

Chapter 4: Setting Goals & Making A Plan 55

Chapter 5: Executing the Plan & Knowing When to Pivot........77

Chapter 6: Vision Control..................................93

Chapter 7: What It Takes to Claim Your Comeback 103

About the Author 115

Bibliography.. 117

FOREWORD

My name is Joseph Luckett, Founder & CEO of Zero to 100 and author of the #1 international bestseller *Zero to 100: The Gold Standard of Global Networking*.

I've known Melissa Jones since 2007, and I am one of her biggest fans, cheerleaders, champions, and supporters. I was so honored and humbled when Melissa asked if I would write the foreword for her book. If you are looking to truly understand what success means and how to arrive at it, this book has the ingredients to make that a reality for you!

The book addresses human vulnerabilities such as facing failure and lacking validation and love. Melissa has not only overcome these vulnerabilities but is also one of the best-qualified people to lead you through the tunnel of failure to the light at the end – SUCCESS!

I could not recommend a better person to learn from, listen to, and engage with. Melissa understands failure and success both on a secular and biblical level. I encourage you to take action in an area of your life that needs change and follow Melissa's lead.

As you read the material, I encourage you to write down everyone that this book could help and send them a message of why they should add it to their library. Let them know they can thank you for it later!

Joseph Luckett
Founder of Zero to 100

PREFACE

I used to struggle with festering resentful thoughts about my life:

"Why must I have such a difficult relationship with my mother?"

"Why do I have to go through so many challenges in my marriage?"

"Why do I have to go through this horrible divorce?"

"Why do I have to be a single parent?"

"Why do I have to experience so much pain, rejection, abandonment, and disappointment?"

I wanted to move forward, grow, and develop into a woman who would have an opportunity to touch many people's lives. I wanted that vision to come to pass in my life so badly that I used to visualize myself speaking on a stage to thousands of people, but I found myself stuck because of the fixed mindset I chose at that time. I had experienced heartbreak to my core, and my fixed mindset had me at a place of stagnancy. Through honesty, humility, and perseverance, I shifted my perspective and overcame the feeling of being stuck with a fixed mindset. As a result, I healed, grew, established healthy boundaries, and became a much more fulfilled version of myself.

For many years, I kept my story of overcoming the trauma caused by abandonment, rejection, and disappointment to myself. But, when I eventually opened up about it, my story ended up encouraging other people who have experienced similar struggles. So now, I find it fulfilling to inspire and help people change their lives for the better.

Not only do I share my story through this book, but I also guide you so you can begin your journey to claim your comeback and live a more fulfilling life. I'll show you how to stop feeling stuck, move from a fixed mindset to a growth mindset, and practically pursue your vision for a better life.

Introduction

CLAIMING MY OWN COMEBACK

Before I dive into how to claim your comeback, I want to share how I came to claim my own. I want you to understand where I came from and how I got to where I am today. I want you to know exactly what I had to come back from so that you know it's possible to overcome some of the most troubling adversity.

MY NEGATIVITY ADDICTION

I don't know where I was, and I don't know what time it was, but I do know it was only by God's irrevocable love and grace that I was able to have a mind transformation that changed the trajectory of my life. I had some deep wounds that I had not figured out how to heal from.

The years I spent battling with emotional, mental, and psychological abuse I had internalized over my life, and being like a foster child no one wanted to be burdened with had taken a toll on me. I swallowed negative feedback as prescribed but kept swallowing until I almost overdosed. I became addicted and tried my hardest to beat this addiction that harmed my mind.

But you see, I wasn't battling the most common addictions to substances such as alcohol and drugs—I was fighting a crippling mindset of negativity. I subjected myself constantly to the thought of not being good enough, regularly dosing on the feeling of not being loved unconditionally and far too many doses of feeling like I was worthless. After decades of attempting to cope with this addiction to these negative thoughts with substitutions for the unconditional love that I so badly sought from essential people in my life, I finally came to a breaking point.

I had a mind transformation!

What does this powerful word mean? Transformation: the word I focused on, which changed my thinking process and ultimately changed my life.

Cambridge defines transformation as "the act or instance of transforming. It's the state of being transformed, a marked change, as in appearance or character, usually for the better."

I wrote this book to help guide you to your transformation.

HOW I REALIZED I NEEDED TO CHANGE

I am such an analytical thinker, and for years I tried to figure out why certain people responsible for molding me were the same ones who contributed to my trauma. I would constantly dwell on the questions: *"Why do they treat me the way they do? How can they be this way and not see it, especially identifying as a Christian?"* I had so many "why" questions, fixating on their behavior and trying to make sense of it.

Bondage and freedom alike start in the mind, and the thoughts we allow to feed either of those mindsets become a stronghold. I was listening to a church sermon one day, and the Pastor said:

"Everything begins with a thought and what you think will get into your heart, what gets into your heart will begin to come out of your mouth, and what comes out of your mouth, you will begin to hear, and what you hear, you'll start to believe, and what you believe, you will begin to possess."

That was the moment the lightbulb went off in my head.

I realized that what you focus on grows. And you just can't make sense of things that just don't make sense.

That's when I finally said to myself, "Okay, Melissa, this situation is like cancer to you. It's time to stop trying to figure it out and get treatment for this potentially deadly disease." I knew the battle to fight this horrific disease would be difficult because, you see, as much as I knew I needed to rid myself of it, I also loved it just as much.

I know you are probably wondering, "who loves a disease?"

Unfortunately, my illness came by way of my bloodline. I believe that many of my relatives, going back for many generations, carried a lot of hurt, disappointments, and trauma from childhood into adulthood.

My realization for my difficult road to recovery was setting boundaries with those who contributed to my trauma. I needed to do what was best for me without an apology.

And that was the foundation on which I came to claim my comeback.

BEFORE MY COMEBACK

I was born in St. Louis, Missouri and raised in East St. Louis, Illinois during the early years of my life. East St. Louis is a small municipality on the eastern side of the Mississippi River in Illinois with a reputation for high poverty and crime rates. I went to a Catholic school from Kindergarten to 4th grade. We then moved to Mid-County St. Louis, where I attended schools in the Ladue School District. With Ladue being the second wealthiest zip code in the Greater Metro St. Louis area, this move was a huge adjustment from the school I had attended previously.

I did alright in school, but it wasn't until college that I excelled academically. I ended up graduating with honors, earning a 3.71 GPA. I attended the Historically Black College and University (HBCU) Alabama A&M University in Huntsville, AL. For my undergraduate work, I majored in Psychology and minored in Sociology. Then I continued my education into grad school by working towards my Master's in School Counseling.

My trauma started in the early years of my life and stemmed from not feeling unconditional love from two critical people: my mother and my biological brother. From an early age, my relationship with them has been complicated. They have never been particularly nurturing or affectionate towards me. I don't recall my brother ever hugging me or even telling me he loved me, nor do I remember my mother saying she loved me until I was in my twenties. Most of the time, I received more criticism from them than praise. After years of feeling so much rejection, I thought it would be best to seek professional counseling to make sense of their behavior. Let me just say, thank God for professional counselors! Through the wisdom and guidance of my counselor, I was able to make sense of the dynamics of at least my mother's behavior for the first time in my life. She handed me the book *Understanding the Borderline Mother: Helping Her Children Transcend the Intense, Unpredictable, and Volatile Relationship*. While reading this remarkable book, I realized my mother had many of the characteristics of a Borderline Mother.

Borderline Personality Disorder (BPD) is a mental health condition characterized by a pattern of instability in moods, behavior, self-image, and functioning. A person with borderline personality disorder may experience intense anger, depression, and anxiety episodes that may last from only a few hours to days. These experiences often result in impulsive actions and unstable relationships. It's estimated that 1.4% of the US adult population has BPD, and of those diagnosed, nearly 75% are women. (Chapman et al., 2021).

At times, the emotional and psychological abuse I experienced from my mother hurt me in ways that took decades for me to make sense of and then heal from. Her actions left a lasting impact and took their toll on me.

When I spent time with my friends and their families, I saw many positive interactions that didn't occur between my mother and me. It made me realize that my relationship with my mother was not the norm, and I began longing for a "normal family."

My biological brother and I were never very close. I believe the division between us was caused mainly by my mother's antics. She blatantly favored my brother. I always got the feeling she saw him as her "golden child." I believe that favoritism pitted my brother against me, resulting in us never building a close bond like siblings should experience. We even got into a physical altercation once as teenagers. The truth is that I wanted a positive relationship with my biological brother and was not afforded that opportunity due to circumstances out of my control. So I tried to cope by finding other relatives – specifically male cousins – to fill that void. It numbed the pain throughout the years and allowed me to cope with the deep grief I felt.

I did the same thing to cope with the lacking relationship with my mother. I've always gravitated to women who I felt could be a mother figure for me. I was closer to some of my father's sisters than my own. There was even a time when I had surgery and reached out to inform my aunt rather than my mother.

I allowed the treatment from my mother and brother to go from affecting me to infecting me. It was like I was drinking poison and waiting for them to die. It wasn't until I was in my thirties that I realized how unhealthy these relationships were. I finally acknowledged that while I couldn't change them, I could not accept their behavior without it infecting me.

I went through so much of my life feeling like I had to prove myself to be loved. It became my natural way of operating and a recurring theme in my relationships. Aside from my mother, who I thought would come around at some point in my journey and recognize my worth and accomplishments, I've experienced this feeling of lacking self-worth within my corporate career.

I am an incredibly driven woman and work hard to accomplish the goals I'm given in my career. I always have that feeling of "I need to prove to my supervisor that I'm worthy of this title." The year 2020 was no different—despite going through a pandemic and being unable to meet with prospects face to face, I met my annual goal for 2020 by October. After reaching my goals, my supervisor told me to take more breaks and ensure I did my best to have a work-life balance, but I struggled to give myself grace. My go-getter mentality intertwines with feeling like I still have to prove myself.

I compensated for not feeling worthy of love by becoming a high achiever and collecting accolades. I was a great athlete through my school years. I played basketball for a few years and ran track all four years of high school, where I competed at the state level and received many medals. I got into CrossFit as an adult and spent a year getting super buff.

Me at the gym in 2015 doing CrossFit training

I was featured in the St. Louis Small Business Monthly February 2020 Publication as "One of the Bankers You Should Know" and have received the Champion Award during my career.

Countless times throughout my life, I've thought to myself, "If I do this, my mother is going to see how valued I am through my accomplishments and finally see that I'm somebody when I've never been anybody to her!"

I was strongly motivated to graduate from college. I was a driven young woman who thought, "What better way to prove my worth to my mother than to be the first person in our immediate family to graduate from college with a Bachelor's degree?"

My biological brother had gone to college but had to end his college career early. I thought I would finally prove worthy to her by finishing school and getting my Bachelor's degree when her golden child didn't.

When I graduated, I was so proud of myself and hoped my mother shared my sentiments. Well, that hope was short-lived because one day after graduation, my mother and I were having a disagreement, and she started comparing me to my biological brother – who made a choice to not complete college and entered the workforce instead.

I said, "At least I graduated from college."

She responded, "Just because you graduated doesn't mean you're smart!"

And that really hurt.

Not only did I graduate Magna Cum Laude in four years with honors and a 3.71 GPA, but I also managed to do so while I was pregnant and becoming a new mother. I got pregnant the summer before my senior year of college and was due the following January.

After giving birth in February of 1998, my parents offered to take my precious newborn baby daughter back home to St. Louis and raise her there until I could graduate from college that May. But I said, "No, I got myself into this situation, and I'll see it through." So I spoke with all my professors, explained the situation, and asked if I could bring my baby to class with me. They all agreed, so I went back to class when she was just seven days old. With my backpack on my back and the pumpkin seat dangling off my arm, I would come to class and sit in the very back just in case she started whining and I needed to step out to console her. Thankfully, she was a great baby who rarely needed consoling. From that point on, my life continued to move like the speed of lightning.

I gave birth to my daughter in February 1998, received my undergraduate degree in May 1998, had a second child in May 1999, and got married in September 1999. Woah, I'm tired just thinking about it, and the train didn't stop there! So when an opportunity arose later in 1999 for me to enter into a banking management program in Cleveland, Ohio, I jumped at the chance. I learned about every aspect of banking and ended up climbing up the corporate ladder. Being a banker was certainly not a part of my plan, but I adjusted my career path to do what I thought was best for my family and myself at that time.

Unfortunately, not long after saying "I do," my marriage was on the rocks, and I decided to return to St. Louis. My ex-husband eventually moved to St. Louis to work on our marriage, and it was during that time we ended up having our third child in March of 2003. My career solidified in St.

Louis when National City Corporation completed an acquisition of Allegiant Bancorp in 2004. I treasured being back in my hometown and near my family, who could be a support system and help me out with my children, but my marriage grew more tense.

Our marriage had become toxic, unhealthy, and abusive. As with many abusive relationships, I justified the behavior and stayed with my ex for much longer than I should have. I was worried I wouldn't be able to provide for my children without the support of a two-parent home and didn't want my children to grow up in a single-parent household.

I finally decided it was time to leave when my ex-husband shattered a mirror by throwing me into it and choking me, followed by the sight of my oldest child running in the bedroom and screaming "Stop it!" at the top of her little lungs. At that moment, I decided that I didn't care if the marriage worked out or not. Separating from him would be better than what my children witnessed in our home.

I consider my most significant accomplishment raising my children as a single mother from the ages of one, five, and six. Shortly after I filed for divorce, my ex-husband moved out of state—so it was just my little ones and me. Now, they are all young adults who are thriving in their endeavors. All three of them are successful. My oldest daughter graduated a semester early from high school, completed her undergraduate studies, received her Bachelor of Liberal Arts degree, and is currently working on her Master's in Kinesiology. My son is working on a degree in

Mechanical Engineering. My youngest is a talented college basketball player pursuing a degree in Sports Management and Physical Therapy. In the US, African American children under 18 who grow up with two married parents (US Population Reference Bureau, 2020) tend to fare better than those who grow up with a single parent (McLanahan & Sandefur, 1996). And my bonus son—Ze'Veyon, who I unofficially adopted in 2019 when he lost his mother unexpectedly—has a Master's degree in Kinesiology and is pursuing a career in the NFL. Considering the statistics, my children have overcome some significant barriers to be successful.

At the time of my divorce, I was deep into my corporate career, and with my children being so young, I had to swallow some pride and reach out to my mother for help. When I was younger, my mother would say quite often, "You'll need me before I need you." She ended up being right about that during this particular season of my life. But I was forced to drop many needed boundaries with her because I needed her support. That lack of planning ultimately came back to bite me.

Although rather painful, I'm grateful that I could rely on her to help me with my children for that period of my life. But as my little ones got older and I didn't need her help as much, my children chose to take advantage of our fractured relationship and played my mother and me against each other.

She would criticize me as a mother, then turn around, overstep her boundaries, and overmother my children. She chose not to understand the struggles I had as a single mother. It felt like she was adding salt to the deep wounds she had caused over the years.

"Melissa, when you have children, you'll understand," my mother would say before I was a mother myself.

Now that I have grown children, her behavior doesn't make any more sense than it did back then. The only explanation is that hurting people hurt people—and I think my mother was really hurting. She has certainly had her own struggles and trauma, which affected how she parented me. This, by the way, is called a Legacy Burden (Earley & Weiss, 2013). I chose to take responsibility for how my traumas affected my behaviors and changed for the better by getting professional help. Unfortunately, my mother decided not to go that route. I believe that a parent must get the proper healing needed to be the best person they can be for their children. You make an effort to heal and move forward—be it for your children or yourself—or you choose not to. Deciding to pick the latter will ultimately cause one to pass hurt down from one generation to the next. Claiming a comeback often means putting a stop to generations of inherited trauma.

FIXED MINDSET VS. GROWTH MINDSET

When I started studying psychology and questioning how one gets stuck in life's ruts, I began to dig into different mindsets. There are two types: a fixed mindset and a growth mindset. Understanding the difference between the two helped me contextualize where I was in my own life.

Before my transformation, I had a fixed mindset. In a *Psychology Today* article by Dr. Michael Puff, he talks about how a fixed mindset is one where people believe their basic skills are fixed traits:

"Now, there's a very important lesson in the difference between fixed mindset versus growth mindset. As parents, it is very important to develop a growth mindset in our kids because if we tell them they're smart or they're stupid and then life changes that, it's going to turn their world upside down.

If we say, 'If you work hard, then you're going to do well, and if you don't work hard, you're not,' that encourages a growth mindset. They can choose not to work hard but it's not because they're either stupid or smart" (Puff, 2017).

People with fixed mindsets often assume that since they have the same DNA as their family, they must have their traits and, therefore, that's how they're going to be. Those with fixed mindsets don't typically want to hear feedback when it's offered, and, as a result, those individuals end up stuck. People with a fixed mindset are constrained by their beliefs and thoughts (Bansal, 2021).

Having a fixed mindset is why I didn't try hard to think outside of the box when I was younger. I felt my talent alone would create success, but as I got older, I started to see the benefit in things like training hard, learning, and developing myself.

When I started to see the potential I had within me by putting in the effort and work, I switched from having a fixed mindset to a growth mindset. A person with a growth mindset is interested in receiving feedback. They want to take something away from constructive critiques so they can grow. For example, a person with a fixed mindset says, "well, if I don't try, I won't fail," but a person with a growth mindset says, "failures are just growth opportunities." After reflecting on my success as an athlete, student, mother, and professional, I finally understood that I was capable of much more.

Once you realize what you are capable of doing, visualize where you would like to be. Next, write down your goals; a goal that's not written down is just a dream. As long as you're willing to learn and put in persistent effort to meet those goals, your growth mindset sets you up for success. As you work through the processes you put in place, you become more capable of navigating the challenges you encounter through this journey called life.

"It's not what happens to you but how you react to it that matters." –Epictetus.

The question that allowed me to shift into a growth mindset was: *How do I continue to look at the glass half full rather than fixating on the negativity and asking, "why me?"*

Instead, I focused on avoiding fixation on the thoughts that upset me and magnified my thoughts on resetting.

WHAT YOU WILL LEARN FROM THIS BOOK

You don't get to choose the circumstances you're born into, and you don't get to decide how you're raised, but despite what happens to you, you can still reach a point of feeling whole and thriving in life.

You truly can learn to live a more fulfilling and successful life. I wrote this book to help you realize that your future isn't determined by what happens to you but by how you respond and navigate life's challenges. No suffering lasts forever. And with the proper guidance and intentionality, you can claim your comeback from whatever you may be going through.

In this book, you will learn how to harness faith to propel you toward mind transformation, how to accept your reality and be grateful for what you have right now, how to identify triggers and traumas that hinder your comeback, how to create and execute SMART plans for your personal life, and how to adjust your vision and claim your comeback.

1

FAITH, HOPE, & YOUR VISION

TAKING THE FIRST LEAP INTO HOPE

The first step in claiming your comeback is finding the hope that you will claim that comeback. Whether you find that hope in your faith, in humanity, or just within yourself, you must connect with it before you can start to transform your mindset.

Hope translates to having a vision. Without a vision, you are more prone to focusing on the negatives. You struggle to picture a better life for yourself. The beacon that lights that picture serves as hope for a better future. While no better future comes overnight, you are allowed to have that hope when you commit to the work that comes with it.

For me, I found that hope through my faith. As a non-denominational Christian, I would frequently look up scriptures that validated how I perceived my life, such as Romans 5:3-4 (English Standard Version):

"...we rejoice in our sufferings, knowing that suffering produces endurance, and endurance produces character, and character produces hope."

People perish because of a lack of knowledge and vision. When you don't have a vision for a better life, you get stuck in simply trying to survive. Faith and hope bring forth that image of a better life. However, that faith does not necessarily need to be solely based on religion. The focus, instead, needs to be on thriving and striving—a growth mindset. There are many paths to mindset transformation, and all that matters is that a vision of a better life comes forth.

"If you fail to plan, you are planning to fail." –Benjamin Franklin.

FAITH AS A BASTION OF HOPE

Even the most faithful among us have days where they get discouraged. We all have days that feel like life has beaten us down. But when you get caught up in toxic ideas that prevent you from having hope, you restrict your ability to be released from that gripping feeling that life has bested you. That's why it's so important to renew your mind and renew it daily.

"Faith is taking the first step even when you don't see the whole staircase." –Martin Luther King Jr.

Faith is "something that is believed especially with strong conviction" (Merriam-Webster).

Hope is "desire accompanied by expectation of or belief in fulfillment" (Merriam-Webster).

You can have faith without having hope. However, having faith can help you when you struggle to have hope.

Faith helps us keep moving forward even when hope is hard to come by. It provides reassurance on your bad days, and it reaffirms your state of mind on good days. Faith helps maintain focus on your vision.

Your faith is only as great as you perceive it to be, and you must exercise it in a manner that's able to serve you. It's like working out. You don't just get fit overnight when you want to get in shape. You have to exercise your muscles and eat right with regularity before seeing results. I exercise my faith by getting up and doing a devotion just about every morning—and it helps me stay true to my vision.

BE WARY OF USING RELIGION TO DENY REALITY

While faith and hope are vital to claiming your comeback, I've learned to be wary of leaning on religion. For me, It's about developing a relationship with God. Addictions arise as a vice to not deal with reality. Religion can have the same numbing or denial effect on reality. Once a person has fallen into that deeply religious mindset, they stop engaging with reality because it can be painful – this is called Spiritual Bypassing. Spiritual Bypassing "describes a tendency to use spiritual explanations to avoid complex psychological issues" (Cherry, 2020). Part of the reason you have to use faith to harness a vision is that it enables you to cope with reality and focus on directing your efforts. For your faith to serve you, you must follow it with accountability and action—or else you're leaning on religion as a means to ignore reality.

For example, I've had exchanges with very religious people who believed they would not catch certain viruses because God would protect them, so they didn't need to take safety precautions. This is a blatant denial of the reality that we are all susceptible to viruses that have the potential to affect our bodies. It disregards the wisdom that God has given us to listen to what doctors and scientists advise to protect ourselves. When you get to the point of blindly putting your trust in your faith without considering what's true, it starts to work against you—and that can be very dangerous.

Individuals who use religion to justify their toxic behaviors repeatedly struggle with the same issues, such as discord in many relationships. They love and believe in God, but they also use religion as a crutch to not deal with reality.

My mother's go-to saying for years was, "just pray, pray, pray," as if that's going to change the dynamics of anything miraculously. I would respond to her, "Yes, prayer definitely is vital, but the Bible also says faith without works is dead." You have to put faith into action to get the results you want to see. You can't just wave a wand and magically will yourself the results you wish to have.

Some may challenge me by saying, "Well, God can do all things." And He most certainly can. However, it's our responsibility to partner with Him, and we don't accomplish that by dismissing our call to action. Reliance on God to resolve everything without taking any action yourself is a rejection of accountability.

I come from a long line of people with Christian values raised in the church. The Bible says, "Honor your mother and father." (Exodus 20:12 New International Version), and throughout my life, my mother has frequently used this verse to justify why she's entitled to use toxic behavior while interacting with me.

In the initial realization of my comeback, I was presented with an opportunity to redefine honor in my faith. I trusted my mother's definition of honor because I felt obligated—she was my mother, after all. But that hurt me. Abiding by her definition of honor caused me to suffer, and I came to realize that I need not compromise joy and fulfillment for the sake of honor.

So as you navigate your comeback, remember that your faith will serve you only if you take responsibility for your actions. Faith without action will blind you and cause you to lose focus of your greater vision.

TRANSFORMATION THROUGH INTENTION

When I immersed myself into CrossFit, my muscles grew over the years, and I thought, "man, this is how people should think of transforming their minds." It is work! If you want to stay in shape and have muscles, you must exercise consistently. It's the same thing with transforming our minds. If we're not intentional about doing the work to change, it will not happen.

An experienced boxer will get knocked out if they don't roll with the punches. The problematic relationship with my mother was painful, but I've since learned to roll with the punches. Now I can anticipate and stop the pattern of hurt within me. If you transform your mind, you become better at rolling with the punches rather than getting knocked out.

You can learn to roll with the punches too. That doesn't mean there won't be pain later on, but that pain will become easier to manage as you grow. You have to commit to that constant development to gain those pain management skills. It's diligent mental work.

As soon as you stop putting in the work and utilizing the tools that it takes to manage hurt, rejection, abandonment, disappointment, or whatever life throws at you, the pain of it all can knock you out. Stay intentional, and the work you put into changing your mindset will pay off.

PUTTING YOUR FAITH TO PRACTICE

I believe we all have a destiny to fulfill. We're all born unique, and we all have our God-given purpose. What trips us up is not knowing that purpose, and sometimes, allowing the people who raise us to project their meaning for our lives onto us. For example, if you have parents who are doctors or lawyers, you may feel obligated to follow in their footsteps. Even if you don't feel like that's your purpose in life, you might follow their path to appease them. You must understand your vision and purpose rather than what someone else wants for you. To claim your comeback, you have to be able to envision success on your terms. Remember, nobody knows your vision except for you and God. We all have a destiny when we're born, and no other human on this earth can tell you what that is. Listen to yourself. Listen to God. What do you really want? Open yourself up to possibility.

Even addicts can claim comebacks. If someone tells me, "I'm a drug addict, and I always will be," I say to them, "Do you desire a better life? Do you recognize that you can have a better life?"

The way towards a better life out of any addiction is by first being honest with yourself. First, you must acknowledge you have a problem. Then you can dig deeper to find the roots of the problem. Asking questions like: "How did I go from being a social drinker to becoming an alcoholic?" and "What is the event that changed the trajectory of my life?" Seldom is it ever the case of someone trying the vice of choice for the first time to see how it would make them feel. There is usually some desire deep down to entertain the feeling of surrendering control. Emotionally stable people want to work through things healthily. It's vital to gain control over your emotions at the start of your healing journey—not surrender control to unhealthy coping mechanisms.

The most important thing to remember is never letting your faith in a better future die. The difference between fulfilled people and those who numb or mask their pain is that they don't allow their hope to be snuffed out. It's not that we don't all have days when we feel hopeless—we're human. But remember, it's just that: a feeling. There are even days when I say out loud, "I kind of feel depressed today." As long as you never let that hope die completely, you are on the right path toward claiming your comeback.

CLAIM YOUR COMEBACK

Here are some questions for you to answer that will help you take the first steps to apply the faith and hope necessary for your transformation:

How do you view yourself?
Describe who you see when you look in the mirror.

_____
_____
_____
_____
_____
_____
_____
_____

Where are you now? Who are you now?

_____
_____
_____
_____
_____
_____
_____
_____

Where do you want to be? What is your vision of a better life?

_____
_____
_____
_____
_____
_____
_____
_____

What is/are your goal(s) to support that vision?

_____
_____
_____
_____
_____
_____
_____
_____

BEGINNING YOUR MIND TRANSFORMATION

Now that you've written down your goals, I want to empower you with wisdom that will help you embrace and overcome life's obstacles. After my many life experiences and research, I have discovered how some people triumph over obstacles and go on to see their goals come to fruition. In contrast, others allow their barriers to break them down and become victims of their circumstances. In my research,

I found one major component that determined how people handled life's obstacles: mindset. As discussed earlier in the book, there's a fixed mindset and a growth mindset. Those who consider themselves victims of their circumstances are often stuck in a fixed mindset. But those who overcome their obstacles and find success have a growth mindset.

Those who operate from a fixed mindset believe that faith alone creates success without effort. We know this to be false because of what God says in James 2:14-17 (The Message):

"Dear friends, do you think you'll get anywhere in this if you learn all the right words but never do anything? Does merely talking about faith indicate that a person really has it?"

Let's say you come upon an old friend dressed in rags and half-starved and say to them, "Good morning, friend! Be clothed in Christ! Be filled with the Holy Spirit!" Then you walk off without providing so much as a coat or a cup of soup. Where does that get you? Isn't it obvious that God-talk without God-acts is outrageous nonsense?

"We can rejoice, too, when we run into problems and trials, for we know that they help us develop endurance. And endurance develops strength of character, and character strengthens our confident hope of salvation." (Romans 5:3-4 New Living Translation).

People who operate with a growth mindset can develop their most basic abilities through dedication and hard work. They understand that brains and talent are just the starting point, and faith is the foundation. This view creates a love of learning and resilience essential for achieving significant accomplishments throughout their lifetime. Growth mindset-focused individuals understand success comes with their willingness to learn, exert effort, and be persistent in meeting their goals. They are apt to see challenges as a natural part of the learning process. They work harder and smarter, which helps them to learn and achieve more than those with a fixed mindset.

"Blessed is the one who perseveres under trial because, having stood the test, that person will receive the crown of life that the Lord has promised to those who love Him." (James 1:12 New International Version).

2

ACCEPTING YOUR REALITY

A home built on an unstable foundation is highly likely to be destroyed. Before you can claim your comeback, you have to face reality. There will be many uncomfortable emotions. You will have to work through these to create a solid foundation for building your comeback.

You simply cannot begin the process of living a fulfilled life until you have faced what's been affecting you so negatively. What traumatic situation triggers you?

It's challenging to accept reality and acknowledge painful truths. It can be one of the most challenging steps in claiming your comeback. But ask yourself this: do you want a better life? If the answer is yes, then ultimately, accepting reality is the only path forward. The issues that caused you to end up where you are in life need to be recognized.

Without recognizing these negative patterns, you're doomed to repeat yourself. If you never got to the root of the issues that caused a former relationship to dissolve, a new partner can trigger responses based on experiences with your old partner. Without seeing and acknowledging these patterns, you're trying to build on an unstable foundation.

Many people make the mistake of thinking they can just suddenly accept reality, and then they'll be fine. But acceptance of truth is not a one-and-done act. Negative patterns are recurring, so acceptance of that reality must be an ongoing process. It's a journey. My negative thought patterns started when I was a little girl. I didn't begin to accept the presence of these negative thought patterns that were reinforced by my relationship with my mother until I was in my thirties. Even then, I felt like I wasn't ready to jump in and change those patterns until I was in my forties. Some people are quicker than others to accept their thought patterns. For me, it took over 20 years. And that's okay! The acceptance process will take as long as you allow it to take, but the most important thing is not to let your hope and vision die.

Remember that it's okay to be afraid of falling back into your old patterns. If accepting reality starts to feel overwhelming, take a breath and slow down. Just dip a toe in until you get comfortable, then ease yourself in slowly.

ACCEPTING REALITY MEANS CHECKING IN WITH YOURSELF

To accept the reality I was in, I had to face the source of my shame and guilt, which meant a lot of trial and error. I made a plan to talk with my mother and set boundaries for her to be in my life. I told her, "I'm going to love you from a distance because your behavior is toxic to me, and I can't allow it to affect me anymore. I'm not taking this step because I want to, but more so because I need to."

Accepting Your Reality

We all need check-ins from time to time. We see doctors for our health, the dentists for our teeth, we check in on our finances with our financial planners, and we even check in on those we care about—but how often do we check in with ourselves?

Acceptance of reality and making progress means consistently checking in with ourselves and making the proper adjustments. I would check in with myself to see how I felt. I would ask myself why I felt bad if I felt off and good if I felt joyful. I took the time to see what was working and what wasn't so I could adjust accordingly.

Taking that time to reflect is of the utmost importance—and instituting that practice in your life will help you come to your acceptance.

* * *

My mother would often respond to my boundary-setting with the same Bible verse over and over again: "Honor your mother and father" (Exodus 20:12 New International Version). I would respond with, "Don't provoke your children to anger" (Ephesians 6:4 New Living Translation). She and I often went around the same merry-go-round when she disagreed with the boundaries I put in place.

My mother typically answered in the same unsatisfying way that she usually did when we had those tough conversations about boundaries: "Well, I'm not perfect, Melissa."

My mother would periodically reach out to me via text when I set my communication boundaries for a season, attempting to break the boundary. She even asked me questions like, "Does God love his children from a distance?"

"By insolence comes nothing but strife, but with those who take advice is wisdom." (Proverbs 13:10 English Standard Version)

THE ATTITUDE OF GRATITUDE

We all have moments of sadness. We all have anxious moments. We wouldn't be human if we didn't have these moments. The beginning of your comeback and acceptance of your reality can often be like a cassette tape—you hit play, and the tape begins to spin across the gears. You're steadily playing through the process of accepting what's real and checking in with yourself to reflect on what you need to move forward. Then all of a sudden—something happens that triggers you to fall back into your negative patterns, and the cassette tape begins to rewind. The trigger to reverse the spin of that cassette tape was often when my mother would send a text and snap me back into my negative thoughts soon after.

To break out of that pattern, I started a gratitude journal. It forced my mind to focus more on the positives than the negatives. Gratitude not only reduces stress but also plays a role in overcoming trauma. One study found that Vietnam War Veterans with higher levels of gratitude experienced lower rates of Post-Traumatic Stress Disorder (Kashdan et al., 2005). Another study found that gratitude contributed to resilience following the terrorist attacks on September 11 (Fredrickson et al., 2003). Recognizing what you are grateful for helps you move away from harboring negativity and towards healing.

What we focus on grows. If I hadn't started journaling, I would have kept hitting that rewind button instead of refocusing my energy and thoughts on more positive things.

Another way you can practice gratitude is by speaking words of affirmation to yourself. Many of us are good at encouraging others, but it's challenging to do it for ourselves. When you get up each day, look in the mirror, tell yourself you're smart, capable, kind, and whatever else you would say to encourage a friend in your shoes. You are your biggest advocate.

ACCEPTING PAINFUL TRUTHS

Owning up to our reality is the first step to becoming unstuck from the fixed mindset patterns holding us back. Accepting reality means stating uncomfortable truths. It's easier for many people to write these uncomfortable truths than to verbalize them, especially when you feel like there's nobody with whom you can speak. Much of my healing came through this writing process. I chose to begin my journal entries with "Dear God..." because, for me, it felt like the best way to get things off my chest without being judged. You're welcome to use this tactic, or you can simply choose to journal to yourself.

This is an important question to answer in coming to terms with reality:

What is something that you are really embarrassed about and fear sharing for the possibility of being judged?

_____
_____
_____
_____
_____
_____
_____

Now, write down what things in your life have been negatively impacting you. These can be burdens that you've taken on, stressors in your life, or circumstances that have made life particularly challenging for you. For example, I would put "not feeling worthy of love" on my list.

List the negative impacts in your life here:

_____
_____
_____
_____
_____
_____
_____

AN EXERCISE IN RELEASING NEGATIVITY

Now that you have your list, pick up a backpack and go outside. Hopefully, the weather is nice today! Collect a big rock or brick for each negative item on your list, attach that negativity to the heavy object, and put it in your bag. Once you have all of the rocks in your backpack, you can feel just how heavy it is to carry the weight of all that negativity. It's important to note that this negativity isn't necessarily stuff you took on yourself—some other people could have thrown rocks in your bag. But at the end of the day, it's still your backpack, and you either decide to carry the weight or remove the weight. The choice is yours to make. That's how stress impacts our body—it's a weight. Even if it's not a physical weight—as it is in this exercise—it's a mental and emotional weight. People threw rocks in my backpack, and I had to take that weight out slowly over the years. You can do the same, but to do so, you must first embrace gratitude.

GRATITUDE PRACTICE

Gratitude is a readiness to show appreciation and to return to kindness. Practicing gratitude is one of the quickest ways to shift your focus away from negativity, judgment, and disappointment. How does one practice gratitude? Start by listing the things in your life for which you are grateful. It doesn't have to be a long laundry list.

You may be thinking, "But I've had a hard life, family challenges, relationship problems, and financial struggles. I can't think of anything I'm grateful for."

If you're struggling to be grateful, I encourage you to set this book down for one minute, go take a look at yourself in a mirror, put your hand over your heart and say out loud to yourself: "I'm breathing and still standing." The fact that you have merely survived is something to be grateful for all on its own.

Now that you completed that exercise and realize you have at least one thing you can be grateful for, let's continue. Beware: one of the worst things you can do when transitioning to a more positive lifestyle is compare yourself to others! Remember that we are all unique and special individuals. God created us to be original, and we should not go through life attempting to be a carbon copy of someone else. Some people have brown eyes, some have hazel, some are right-handed, some are left-handed, some have athletic talent, and some have musical talent. God made us all perfect in our uniqueness. He is the potter, and we are the clay.

"You made my whole being; you formed me in my mother's body. I praise you because you made me in an amazing and wonderful way. What you have done is wonderful. I know this very well." (Psalm 139:13-14 New Century Version)

God's Word says He made our whole being—not just 25%, not just 50%, not just 99%—He made our whole being. God made 100% of our being, so we know we were made exactly how we were supposed to be made. So, the challenge is not how we were made but how we see ourselves.

Most of the Book of Psalms was written by King David, whose life was filled with much pain. He had many opportunities not to be grateful. But as you can read in this Psalm, he says, "I praise you because you made me in an amazing and wonderful way."

You may have had a difficult upbringing; you may have experienced rejection; you may have experienced abandonment; you may not have received the genuine love you needed from certain people in your life. But you can always choose to be grateful for what you do have. We can learn a lot from King David.

If you are not a believer of God and prefer a more secular approach to justifying your attitude of gratitude, I refer you back to the importance of perspective. No matter what you have been through, you're never at a complete loss. There are always positive and uplifting things that you can be grateful for.

Research supports the practice of gratitude as having a positive impact on our health. Even for those with controlling personalities, gratitude can increase psychological well-being (Lin, 2015), make us more resilient (Birnbaum & Friedman, 2014), give us higher self-esteem (Rash et al., 2011), and even keep suicidal thoughts at bay for those who are stressed and depressed (Krysinska et al., 2015). Simply journaling for five minutes a day about what we are grateful for can enhance our long-term happiness by over 10% (Seligman et al., 2005).

In this next exercise, I would like you to list things you are grateful for. It can be anything, big or small.

1. _____
2. _____
3. _____
4. _____
5. _____
6. _____
7. _____
8. _____
9. _____
10. _____

Take this practice one day at a time. Be intentional about checking in with yourself. Gratitude is harder to come by some days more than others. Don't get discouraged if things don't progress as fast as you wish. Be mindful that events could change the trajectory of the vision you've set for yourself. Whatever comes up, positive or negative, take note and stay the course of practicing gratitude.

3

IDENTIFYING ROADBLOCKS & TRIGGERS

OVERCOMING OBSTACLES

When you hear the word "obstacle," what do you think about? What do you envision? Many view obstacles as something that stands in the way or holds up progress. It's a person or thing that hinders something—an obstruction designed or employed to disrupt or block the movement of an opposing force. Obstacles can be natural, manufactured, or a combination of both.

As you'll recall about the chapter on mindsets, some people handle obstacles as if the road they are traveling has come to an end—with no forks in the road, no detours, no bridges to drive over, or overpasses to drive under that lead them to another street. But some use obstacles to learn, grow, and come closer to their goals in life. They persevere through some of the most challenging moments in life, remaining constant to their God-given purpose in the face of obstacles and discouragement. The time has come to pursue your goals despite obstacles or opposition.

So you've begun to ground yourself in belief, faith, hope, foster a growth mindset, and also come to accept the reality you're in. The next phase in claiming your comeback is identifying what's holding you back from progress.

Which relationships are toxic and hinder your progress?

What specifically triggers you to slip away from progress?

For me, engaging with my mother on her terms was a trigger. Our relationship without boundaries was toxic and hindered me from progress. I once managed to set boundaries with my mother when I was married. At that time, I struggled with her coming to my house unprompted and buying my children junk food—it was already hard enough to regulate the amount of unhealthy food the kids were eating. So, I told her she needed to let me know when she would be coming over and stop buying them junk food. During that season of my life, I could set that boundary. But, when I found myself going through a divorce, I was met with a tough decision. As my ex-husband moved out of state, I struggled to balance being a newly single mother with three little kids while working a corporate 9 to 5 job. So for the sake of my children's well-being, I reached out for her help—and I ended up needing to depend on her support for many years while raising them. It took a lot to put my pride aside and do what was best for my children at that time. It's typically when someone has too much pride that things get worse.

"Pride goes before destruction and a haughty spirit before a fall." (Proverbs 16:18 New International Version)

Identifying Roadblocks & Triggers

As difficult as that decision was, I'm grateful to God for helping me put my pride and vulnerability aside by allowing her back into my life. As I've matured and navigated through life, I have realized that pride makes excuses, but humility makes adjustments. I needed to humble myself to make the necessary adjustments in order to claim my comeback.

When making decisions that serve your greater vision, your vision has to supersede your emotions. You have to take your feelings out of the decision-making process. For me, this often meant making a pros and cons list. When I could look at my list and say, "this is what makes the most sense even though I don't want to do it," I knew I was on the right path. I determined that temporarily dealing with toxic and triggering behaviors from my mother to get through my divorce and single motherhood was the right decision for my children and me.

You have to put those logical needs over what you want to meet the vision you have for yourself. We all have to make sacrifices for our vision and continue to ask ourselves: How badly do I want this?

When I filed for divorce, my vision was to raise my children the way I desired. I wanted to put them through schools with high academic ratings and position them to be the best and most successful people they could be in life. I couldn't put my feelings and my pride ahead of what I wanted for them, so I had to do what I needed to do to make sure that vision came to pass—and that meant forgoing some healthy boundaries with my mother.

She did indeed help take pressure off by providing support as their grandmother. I raised my children to understand that you never fail if you learn from a situation, but if you continue to find yourself in the same position without changing how you respond, there's a high likelihood of the same outcome.

While I needed my mother's support for my children during that vulnerable season of my life, I learned that valuable lesson from the experience of compromising my boundaries with her. Eventually, I ended up setting boundaries with her again. (More on that in Chapter 5).

TRACING THE ROOTS OF TRIGGERS AND TRAUMAS

The obstacles that you find repeatedly crossing your path on the way to your comeback are rooted deeply in traumatic experiences. Our unhealed trauma causes us to do one of three things: fight, flee, or freeze. I chose to fight!

Some people might decide to flee by avoiding pressure or challenges. Others might decide to freeze, staying stagnant and stuck in the same circumstances year after year. These are trauma responses triggered by real-life situations.

To uproot and heal from these traumas, you have to trace what triggers you so that you can heal. Tracing these triggers will help you move past becoming a fighter, fleer, or freezer into the ideal state: flow. To flow, you have to be willing to process your traumas. If you can recognize your trauma, you can identify the triggers because triggers cause us to repeat negative behaviors.

My mother and father have been married for over 50 years, so my mother has never had the experience of parenting alone. My parents both worked outside of the home, but they also had help from my grandparents and an uncle who fed us breakfast and took us to school each morning. My mother also never had the experience of being a single mother, yet I felt harsh judgment from her being a single mother.

That's a large part of why I resist passing judgment on anybody—I don't want to display any characteristics that can be perceived as hurtful. I want to understand as much as I can before coming to a conclusion about someone's choices. Somebody can be smoking crack, and my instinctual reaction is, "Oh my goodness, what happened? What happened to you to get here? What has hurt you? What traumatic situation has led you here?"

My tendency towards withholding judgment eventually made me curious about my mother. She was always so private and secretive with me, while I strive to be open and honest with my children. Eventually, I learned that she had been through things in her life that catalyzed her issues.

I discovered later in life that my mother's father—who I knew but wasn't close to—left my grandmother with whom he had four children. My mother was the oldest of the four. He started a relationship with another woman out-of-state and then had a daughter who he seemed to favor much more than my mother and her siblings. I believe my mother longs for something from her father she never received.

I never witnessed my parents express affection for one another. From my perspective, it seems my mother didn't get what she was longing for from the men in her life, so she ended up gravitating toward my brother. Then when my brother got married, she started to gravitate toward my son Ajay.

That's when I had a lightbulb moment.

They're called "generational curses." If we dig deep into our family history, we can find a common link. The Gospel Coalition describes a generational curse as "the cumulative effect on a person of things that their ancestors did, believed or practiced in the past, and a consequence of an ancestor's actions, beliefs, and sins being passed down" (Makashinyi, 2019). These are also known as a "legacy burden" by therapists who work with the Internal Family Systems Model (Earley & Weiss, 2013). Many of us develop "inner critics," and some model this critic off of a parent.

In my case, that burden was passed down through my mother and I, too, had a void that I sought to fill from lacking her validation and praise. As a kid, I had a bad temper and started fighting a lot in school. Once, a girl called me the B-word, and I just started hitting her. If I wasn't so angry with my mother and brother at home, I don't think fighting would have been my first reaction. But because I felt rejection from my family that caused me trauma, that girl calling me the B-word girl in school triggered me.

I decided to express my insights with my mother to get closer and share some understanding.

Identifying Roadblocks & Triggers

Her response?

"Well, I'm glad you were able to diagnose me, Melissa."

While this response was disheartening, it helped affirm that I was doing the right thing by addressing my issues and getting the help I needed not to repeat her behavior. I decided to be the generational curse breaker and stop the inheritance of these deeply buried hurt feelings.

Prayerfully, my kids have lived a life where they don't have to decipher what their mother really means, as I did with my mother. I tell my kids like it is, or as their generation says, I "keep it 100." I want my children to have a mother who constantly strives to be a better version of herself. I believe I have done that by identifying my roadblocks, traumas and triggers, setting boundaries, and making intentional and gradual improvements.

Whether you're trying to claim your comeback for yourself or your children, there's an undeniable benefit in striving to be a better version of yourself. Although confronting triggers and traumas is a painful and ongoing process, it's a necessary means for moving forward. It's the price we pay for a better life. Chemotherapy is a brutal treatment that wreaks havoc on the human body, but it does treat cancer and, many times, kills cancerous cells. Confronting these deeply rooted traumas will be painful, but it will keep you from continuing to suffer, feeling stuck in your life and mindset.

Trauma is like a weed. If you don't pull it out by the root, it's going to grow back.

A LESSON ON TRIGGERS & ROADBLOCKS

It's essential to not only listen to those who have overcome challenges and come out on the other side, but also really listen to yourself. There's a difference between hearing and listening. You can hear anything, but it takes focus and understanding to listen—even if it's to listen to that small, still voice within us that tells us not to go down the path of negativity.

If you suffer a consequence from a poor choice then beat yourself up for it, that negativity compounds on itself. Be wise and acknowledge triggers as they arise to avoid going down that rabbit hole.

Here are my methods for avoiding going down the rabbithole:

1. Focus

Stay on the course of your vision and recognize when a trigger is forcing you off course.

Despite any progress you make, a trigger always has the potential of sucking you back into your old thought patterns. Instead of allowing yourself to get sucked in, acknowledge that a negative thought pattern is arising, accept it, and ask yourself what you can do to tweak the impact it's going to have on you.

2. Take Action

Minimize the impact that triggers have by setting boundaries.

Remember that this is a process and that when triggers arise, the point is not to squash their impact, but to minimize their effects. To prevent your triggers from having so much influence, set boundaries.

3. Make Tweaks

Setting boundaries that minimize the impact your triggers have on you is a process that requires tweaks over time. They don't need to be sweeping changes.

Small, gradual changes are far more manageable and sustainable than sweeping changes. You will need to make adjustments to the boundaries that you set. You may find that you need different boundaries at different times or that previously-set boundaries just aren't serving you in the way you thought they would. It's all a part of the ongoing process to find what works for you in minimizing the impact of trauma.

One day when I found myself going down the rabbithole, I realized that indulging myself in this negativity was like drinking poison and wanting my mother to die. I couldn't control her, but I could control how I responded to her. Ultimately, I decided I wanted to stop drinking the poison and just pour it out instead.

You don't have control over who or what triggers you and what traumatic events have occurred in your life. But you do have control over how you respond to those triggers and traumas.

DO YOU SEE WHAT I SEE?

In this next exercise, you will have an opportunity to gain perspective on your mindset. Have you been viewing triggering situations from a fixed or growth mindset?

First, write down a situation that triggered you, and to which you didn't respond well.

Then, you will describe your response to that situation and the decision you chose to make based on that response.

The goal at the end of the exercise is to see the situation from a different perspective.

Situation:

_____
_____
_____
_____
_____
_____
_____
_____

Your Response:

_____
_____
_____
_____
_____
_____
_____
_____

Your Decision:

_____
_____
_____
_____
_____
_____
_____

Now, taking the same situation and applying what you've learned so far, let's explore how you could have chosen to respond more positively.

Remember the beginning of the chapter when I talked about how some people look at obstacles as if the road they're traveling on has come to a dead-end? Then, you have the others who used their obstacles to learn and grow so they could move much closer to their goals in life.

How could you have responded differently if you were using this same situation as an opportunity to learn and grow?

Your Decision:

_____
_____
_____
_____
_____
_____
_____
_____

Positive Decisions:

_____
_____
_____
_____
_____
_____
_____

Now you can hopefully see the difference between a positive and a negative approach to controlling your response and decisions. Put these tools into practice and apply them to all uncomfortable situations in your life.

TAKING THE EMOTION OUT OF DECISION-MAKING

To make decisions that serve your greater vision, you need to remove emotional reactivity from the process. I recommend making a pros and cons list. Think of a difficult situation you are currently faced with and take the opportunity to note the benefits and drawbacks to each possible course of action. By the time you've worked through it, you should better understand which decision is best aligned with your vision.

Identifying Roadblocks & Triggers

POSSIBLE DECISION #1:

_____

PROS

_____
_____
_____
_____
_____
_____
_____
_____

CONS

_____
_____
_____
_____
_____
_____
_____
_____

POSSIBLE DECISION #2:

_____

PROS

_____
_____
_____
_____
_____
_____
_____
_____

CONS

_____
_____
_____
_____
_____
_____
_____
_____
_____

Identifying Roadblocks & Triggers

POSSIBLE DECISION #3:

PROS

CONS

Over time, you will find that shifting your response helps your mindset shift as well. Practicing this mindset will yield growth over the obstacles that stand in your way. In the next chapter, I will discuss how to create an action plan for your shifting mindset.

4

SETTING GOALS & MAKING A PLAN

"For if anyone is a hearer of the word and not a doer, he is like a man who looks intently at his natural face in a mirror. For he looks at himself and goes away and at once forgets what he was like. But the one who looks into the perfect law, the law of liberty, and perseveres, being no hearer who forgets but a doer who acts, he will be blessed in his doing." (James 1:23-25, English Standard Version)

While having the ability to identify sources of negativity in your life—knowing your triggers and roadblocks—is imperative to claim your comeback, it's not enough on its own to move you forward. Without action, you fall back into a fixed mindset. That's why you must make a SMART plan to hold you accountable to a growth mindset.

SMART is an acronym that has been used in the corporate management world for decades. It's commonly attributed to Peter Drucker's "Management by Objectives" concept dating back to the 1950s (Drucker, 2006). However, the first known use of the term was in the November 1981 issue of Management Review by George T. Doran.

I learned about SMART goals early in my career during training in my corporate job. Much of the training seemed excessive. For example, I could have done without learning how to shake someone's hand. However, I understand why they taught us about SMART goals and how I could benefit from putting them to practice.

Let's break it down:

S —Specific
Goals should be simple and straightforward.

M –Measurable
You should be able to track your progress.

A –Achievable/Attainable
Goals should be realistic and reasonable.

R –Relevant
Goals should be worthwhile, fair, and executed at the right time.

T –Time-bound
Your goals should have a deadline and a timeline.

Setting SMART goals has helped me hold myself accountable for the progress I've sought to make throughout my career. By setting up annual goals that I break down into smaller, bite-size weekly goals, I can often achieve my professional goals ahead of schedule. Despite 2020 being a year of navigating through a pandemic, where meeting face to face with clients and potential clients became obsolete, I was not only able to achieve my annual goals by October but exceeded them by year-end. It's truly a valuable tool for growth and progress—not just in a professional setting. Taking the time to think through and write down SMART goals in our personal lives can be just as helpful.

Setting Goals & Making a Plan

Personal SMART goal setting is a way to hold yourself accountable and see yourself making progress. You can even apply SMART goals to how you set boundaries—be those boundaries with a toxic individual in your life, limits with alcohol or drugs, or boundaries in a mindset issue you're struggling with. This is a strategy to measure weaning yourself off of it, practically whatever your vice is.

Plus, let's face it: if you don't have a plan, the chances are that you will fall back into the same old habits.

If you fail to plan, well, you're really just planning to fail.

With healing from personal matters, we often try to reinvent the wheel. There's a practice called ECT (Electroconvulsive Therapy), where small electrical currents cause brief triggers which can change brain chemistry. A study has shown that ECT can reverse certain mental health conditions (van Buel et al., 2017). That may be a partial fix, but we simply cannot wipe our memories clean like a hard drive. We are not computers. Even if someone has gone through that therapy and successfully minimized the effects of their triggers, they still would not have processed and healed from the trauma roots of the trigger. What's needed is long-term habit-changing strategies that support our healing.

The tools we apply to progress in our professional lives also work just as well in our personal lives. SMART plans are great for breaking patterns because they break down big goals into bite-size goals then hold us accountable for taking action.

MAKING GOALS SPECIFIC

When you make a SMART goal, specificity is crucial. If it's not specific enough, you risk entirely falling off track of your plan. A goal that isn't specific enough is just a dream or a wish.

Example: When it was time to set a boundary around my mother coming over unannounced, I set a goal to change my garage code within 30 days. This goal was specific enough for me to act on, and it fulfilled the boundary I needed.

MAKING GOALS MEASURABLE

We struggle with progressing towards our comebacks because we fail to set up checkpoints to ensure we're on the right path. When you make a SMART goal, making it measurable prevents you from setting intentions and blindly acting on them without a measuring stick to track your progress. Measurability can also keep you from prolonging or delaying progress toward your goal.

Example: I worsened the situation when my mother sent me frustrating texts, and I didn't take a moment to assess how to respond. So I set a measure to not respond to her within the following seven days. Sometimes I would go longer without responding or not even respond at all. Over time, the texts from her slowed down. This measure deescalated the communication and helped taper my negative responses to my mother.

MAKING GOALS ACHIEVABLE/ATTAINABLE

If you're ambitious like I am, you often want to shoot for the moon. When setting a SMART goal, that's not something you can do. You need a plan that is reasonable enough for you to accomplish. You need something achievable to lead you toward your greater goal of healing—not to discourage you because it's too challenging.

Example: Ideally, I would have liked to have set a boundary where I didn't have to communicate with my mother as often as I had to, but that was just not attainable. She had a relationship with my children, and we went to the same church. Because zero communication wasn't reasonable, I told her that I needed to love her from a distance. I explained that this meant she was not welcome in my home, and the extent of our in-person communication would be an exchange of pleasantries. She didn't believe I was serious about this boundary and continued to try to push back at it.

MAKING GOALS RELEVANT

SMART goals need to be set at the right time, matching your present needs, and you also need to have the right resources for a plan to be relevant enough to achieve. If a goal is not appropriate enough, it can stop you from pursuing it atogether.

Example: If I had not made my initial SMART goal relevant to my situation, I might still allow my mother to overstep boundaries. It would have likely taken me more time, effort, and intention to claim my comeback.

MAKING GOALS TIME-BOUND

You make a SMART goal time-bound simply by setting a deadline. While you may not achieve your goal by that deadline, by selecting one, you still have an intention to review and make tweaks to your SMART plan. When you don't make a goal time-bound, you lose a significant measure of accountability to yourself, sabotaging your comeback.

An advantage of having a goal be time-bound is that it prevents the goal setter from using the excuse of "life happens" to deprioritize the SMART goal. While life is happening, having a plan that you want to accomplish, especially when removing yourself from toxic situations or setting boundaries with toxic people—like I had to do for my comeback—you still have to make it a priority. Without proper balancing of priorities, everyday tasks start to take precedence over that goal.

Example: I gave myself a deadline of 30 days from when I set the goal.

KEEP YOUR FOCUS FORWARD

There's a reason we have a big front windshield and a small rearview mirror. A rearview mirror is smaller because you need to know what's behind you without focusing on it. You can't drive your car looking in the rearview mirror. If you do, you will most certainly crash. Instead, focus on what's in front of you because that's what you are moving toward. You only need to glance at what's behind you every so often to maintain awareness and perspective.

But why is it so tempting to look out of the rearview mirror? Because focusing on the past is more manageable—it's what we already know. We don't know about the future, and that can be scary.

"It's not in the pursuit of happiness that we find fulfillment, it is in the happiness of pursuit." –Denis Waitley

We're not pursuing happiness; we're seeking fulfillment. To do that, we have to be able to flow through life's ups and downs. You'll have difficult seasons, but you just have to know "that all things work together for good to them that love God, to them who are the called according to his purpose." (Romans 8:28 King James Version).

I used my faith to help me move forward, pull my focus away from the rearview mirror, and instead look at what was in front of me. Faith looks forward!

A story about Joshua leading the Israelites over the Jordan River in the Bible resonates with me. He was trying to bring a large group of what I could imagine were negative people with him and was very focused because God had appointed him to get the people across that river. Negativity will continue to arise in our lives, but we must always remain focused on getting to our destination. We don't get to choose what rivers we will cross in our own lives. We can't decide which obstacles will cross our paths or what traumatic events we may face. Life happens. But, what we do get to determine is what we carry with us while crossing the river.

If you want to cross a river and enter the next season of your life healed, healthy, and whole, you can't carry so much baggage. When I crossed the river to the new season of my life, I realized that I couldn't bring the hurt that I had experienced with me. I knew that it would take longer to cross the river if I held onto that pain, abandonment, disappointment, and rejection. You, too, have to understand what to let go of so you can cross the river when it's time. ***What rocks were you carrying in your backpack from the exercise in Chapter 2?***

I believe God wants you to partner with Him so that you can live an abundant, fulfilled life. It's imperative to allow your faith to move you forward, but you must put action behind your prayers. The Bible says faith without works is dead. If you can get to the middle of the river, He will see you and meet you there. God has helped you get to the other side before—and that's where your faith comes in. Faith and prayer keep us going through our SMART plans.

VIRUSES ARE CONTAGIOUS

Just like with any virus—you can catch a negative thought that multiplies and infects you. The negative ideas that infected my mind were harmful thoughts from my mother, such as:

"You graduated from college, but that doesn't make you smart."

"You're not going to blame me for the way you turned out."

Setting Goals & Making a Plan

On my healing journey, there were times when I would ask myself, "Where did all these weak thoughts come from? I am a *strong* person!" These thoughts led to me *feeling* weak, and I had to take the time to recognize where those thoughts came from—because what you don't acknowledge, you tacitly encourage.

The source of our negative thoughts determines where these thoughts will lead us if we don't actively change the thought patterns. That's why you see alcohol abuse, drug addiction, physical abuse, and emotional abuse occur; it all starts with a thought—thoughts that get out of control. You have to ask yourself: What's at the core of these thoughts so that I can address them adequately?

As I said in Chapter 3, we may not control what other people say or do to us, but we can control our responses to people. Having this perspective and making a concerted effort to apply it more to my own life, I found myself pausing when I'd say, "she makes me *so angry!*" She wasn't *making* me feel anything. Those were *my thoughts* and responses. It took time for me to understand the concept that everything within me began with a thought before I caught any feelings. I knew since it started with a thought—*"she offended me once again"*—an attitude of frustration would habitually follow.

Feeling frustration as a response to someone else's actions is natural human behavior. That frustration becomes unhealthy when you allow the feelings to compound, leading to a sense of insecurity and victimization of your judgment.

It's a domino effect that leads to the use of whatever vices help us cope with those insecurities.

Remember the words of a pastor's sermon I heard from earlier in the book: *"What you think will get into your heart as a feeling, what gets into your heart eventually finds its way out of your mouth, and when it finally makes its way out of your mouth and into the atmosphere, a battle begins."*

You have to choose which side of the battle you're going to fight on. Are you going to succumb to your intrusive thoughts and the vices you use to cope (ex., drinking out of control, doing drugs, or feeding on negativity), or are you going to fight against those unhealthy patterns with a SMART plan?

SETTING MY FIRST PERSONAL SMART GOAL

When I decided to claim my comeback, it was vital to thrive internally and not just survive. Before my comeback, I felt like I was thriving in my personal and professional life, but I was just surviving inside. I was still hurting so much from the disappointments and rejection I experienced for so many years. It was to the point that I felt uncomfortable being at family functions and sharing space in a room with people who had hurt me in a way I hadn't healed from.

I realized that if I didn't reconcile my trauma, it would just get worse. Even if that trauma lay dormant for years, it could come back—almost like cancer. So my initial SMART goal came from the need to control my response to my mother and set up boundaries.

Sometimes we try to minimize truths that hurt us to cope with the complex emotions. When I started my healing journey, despite having the intention to heal, I dealt with my hurt by pretending I didn't care about the behavior that hurt me. But I can say now that their lack of interest in having a healthy relationship with me was painful. And I could not control their lack of interest. However, I could control my response to them and how I would heal.

Here's how I made my initial big personal goal into a SMART one:

Specific with Intention to Change my Response

I intended to heal from the hurt, and that road to healing started specifically with me not allowing myself to respond to her actions negatively. When she would do something that bothered me, my gut reaction was to call her out, spiraling into an argument. Much of the time, she would hang up on me, which resulted in more tension later on. It was a vicious cycle. I knew if I could get to a place of not responding so negatively to what I considered manipulative behavior, I would be in a healthier place.

Measurable by Counting Days without Negative Responses

When I set this goal, I heard it took 21 days to change a habit, so I decided not to react to my mother for 21 days. I figured that if I could do it for that long, I would have less of an urge to respond negatively to her at all. Once I hit the 21-day mark, I would stretch the goal and try to do it for another 21 days, and so on.

Achievable to Not Have a Negative Response

Healing entirely from my trauma was not a reasonable goal to start with, but it did make sense to start with the more attainable goal of training knee-jerk negative responses out of myself. The goal was realistic, but it also had some heavy constraints because I depended on my mother to help me with my children when they were young. I couldn't just say that I wasn't going to deal with her at all. As time moved forward, I adjusted this goal as my two oldest children became adults, and my youngest was nearly a young adult. They no longer needed to depend on her as much. Therefore, neither did I.

Relevant by Directly Contributing to Healing from this Toxic Relationship

As I said about my goal being achievable, initially, not dealing with my mother was not an option. I needed her back then, so I needed to work on my healing within the bounds of those needs until I wasn't dependent on her and I could set stricter boundaries. It was the right time to begin the healing process, but it was not the right time for the SMART plan that I adopted later—which involved far more control around interacting with her.

Time-Bound by the Deadline I Set for Myself

I took the 21-day timeline that I was using to measure my progress to time-bind my SMART goal. If I slipped up and responded negatively at any point in those 21 days, I would start over until I could make it to 21 days in a row.

By making my goal a SMART goal, I went from immediately reacting with frustration to her to pausing and saying out loud to myself, "oh, here she goes again." I trained myself not to be shocked by her behavior and continue without having a negative response.

At one time, I felt guilty about setting boundaries. But once I understood that blocking out petty arguments with my mother was only a temporary solution for my healing. It helped me manage my response, but I realized I couldn't reach my next goal without hard conversations.

Healing through Hard Conversations

Someone suffering the consequences of a fixed mindset in toxic relationships—as I did—often needs to arrive at a place in their healing journey where they can have a conversation with the individual or individuals who have hurt them.

Knowing the difference between what is affecting you versus infecting you will be the key to your healing process. When you allow the actions of others to infect you, that's when you will find yourself most out of control. I struggled to eradicate that infection because those who inflicted trauma wouldn't have the challenging but necessary conversations with me.

I initially SMART-planned to have these tough conversations with my mother. I thought if I had a better understanding of her thought process and why she did it, it would help my healing process. But I soon realized that I would not get that information from her. She just wasn't willing to give me the answers I felt I needed to heal, so I had to go back and edit my healing plan when it became evident I wouldn't heal through conversation with her. And despite not getting the answers I wanted at that time, it was part of my healing process.

However, writing this book and asking my mother questions she was willing to answer provided me with more clarity than I ever had. She said that if she could go back and parent me differently, she'd have had more open communication, expressed more love, and disciplined me differently. She also admitted to overstepping boundaries as a grandparent and learning from her mistakes. She didn't acknowledge, though, the difference in how she treated my brother. She claimed that she didn't remember several examples of misaligned treatment I spoke about, but in any case, this was far more honesty than I had ever received from her before.

Talking with my brother was also part of my healing SMART plan. I called him years ago asking to meet for lunch and talk through some things that occurred throughout our lives.

"I'm working seven days a week right now," he responded.

"Oh, I get it. My schedule is really busy, too," I replied.

He was married with one child and a busy job. I was a single parent in a corporate job with three children at home—so I did understand what it was like to have a busy schedule. I told him that I thought this was important, but what I didn't tell him was that "you make time for what's important... and you have to eat."

I asked him to let me know when he was available, but he never did. He never afforded me the time to have a conversation, yet when I would see him once or twice a year at family functions, he would just say, "what's up?" to me as if he hadn't blown me off. It was painful to come to terms with the fact that I wouldn't get the answers that I felt I needed from him either.

The healing that people need from experiences like these frequently happens through communication with those who have hurt us. But speaking with those individuals is not a fix-all solution. We still have to work through our healing process, realizing that we've allowed that hurt from someone else to infect us and recognizing that we already have happiness lying dormant within us. That's why when these conversations don't happen, we are not at a complete loss for healing. We can still heal without these conversations—we can still move forward without that closure.

It's like having a goal to bake a cake, and the recipe calls for 2% milk, but you only have skim milk. The cake may not taste the same, but you will still have achieved the goal of baking a cake if you use skim milk.

ALTERNATIVES TO HEALING THROUGH CONVERSATION

Those who are unable to have conversations with the people who have hurt them—or like me, who were unable to get the answers they felt they needed through conversations—need to find other healthy outlets as a means for healing. For me, the Bible was a source of healing. I started journaling to God and wrote all of my feelings out. That was a way to healthily release all that built-up anger I had suppressed. This journaling strategy works for people who don't hold a belief in a higher power, too. It's a very healthy alternative if talking it out isn't an option or doesn't feel safe.

Some people feel like hitting a punching bag releases those emotions. Journaling is almost like hitting a punching bag for me. It's a healthy release for the negative thoughts—which risk looping on repeat if there are no healthy release options. When we don't release the negativity, our minds will keep replaying it, especially when something triggers that deeply held traumatic experience.

APPLYING SMART GOALS TO YOUR COMEBACK

Don't go through life feeling like you're on a sailboat allowing the wind to push you in whatever direction it blows. Make the vital choice of charting a course and controlling where your boat goes. SMART goals can do that for you.

Now it's time for you to make a SMART goal in an area of your life where you feel you need to heal. Remember, you must write down your SMART plan. A goal or vision that's not written down is just a wish or dream. You must not only know what a SMART goal is, but you also must know how to use SMART goals for them to be effective. I may understand what tools a plumber uses, but I don't know how to use them—that makes me a pretty useless plumber! So let's help you understand how to use these tools.

First, start by writing out a general goal you have in contributing to your healing process:

_____
_____
_____
_____

Now, let's make that goal a SMART one. Remember:
S —Specific
M -Measurable
A -Achievable/Attainable
R -Relevant
T -Time-bound

Getting SPECIFIC

It helps to answer "W" questions to get more specific:
What do you want to accomplish? **Who** is involved?
Why is your goal important? **Where** is it located?
What resources are required? **What** are the limitations?

Ex. When I was more dependent on my mother to help my children, that limited me in my boundary setting because I needed her.

_____
_____
_____
_____

So, what specifically do you want to accomplish in one sentence?

Ex. My specific intention in my initial SMART goal was to stop myself from negatively responding to my mother.

_____
_____
_____
_____

Making It **MEASURABLE**

How will you know when your goal is accomplished? How much? How many?

Ex. I decided my goal once was accomplished when I made it 21 days without responding negatively to my mother.

_____
_____
_____
_____

Making it **ACHIEVABLE**

Remember that you can only control what you can control. People or situations may prevent you from achieving what you consider ideal. You won't feel successful in accomplishing your goal unless you recognize the constraints around your plan from the start. Therefore, you need to design this goal with those limitations in mind. Remember that you can adjust these goals later as the constraints change!

How realistic is the goal based on the current situational constraints? How can you make this goal reasonable enough to accomplish?

Ex. Because I depended on my mother when my children were young, I knew a goal of cutting her out was not achievable. Working within my constraints, I made my goal attainable by focusing on what I could control: changing my response to her.

_____
_____
_____
_____

In one sentence, state how your goal is achievable:

Ex. I will change my response to my mother.

_____
_____
_____
_____

Staying **RELEVANT**

Is now the right time for this goal?

Ex. Not dealing with my mother wasn't an option when I set my first personal SMART goal. My circumstances have since changed, and now is the right time for the more robust

SMART plan that I have—to maintain a strict boundary around communication, not allowing her to overstep those boundaries that I put in place.

So, is it the right time for this goal? Does this goal match your needs? Is it doable in your current environment? Does it seem worthwhile?

_____
_____
_____
_____

TIME-Binding Your Goal

When I set my first SMART goal, I read that it took 21 days to change a habit, so I time-bound my goals to 21 days. Today, studies show it can take anywhere from 18 to 254 days for a person to form a new habit and an average of 66 days for a new behavior to become automatic (Gardner et al., 2012). So keep that in mind when you're time-binding your own goals.

What can you do today/immediately to achieve your goal(s)? What can you do 66 days from now? What can you do six months from now?

_____
_____
_____
_____

Setting Goals & Making a Plan

To simplify things, in one sentence, state what the deadline is for this goal:

Ex. By the time 21 days have passed, I will have changed my response to my mother.

_____
_____
_____
_____

5

EXECUTING THE PLAN & KNOWING WHEN TO PIVOT

Having faith that you can move toward your vision while accepting the reality you're in presently is incredibly valuable. Identifying obstacles while working toward that vision and having an intentional SMART plan to navigate those obstacles is even more helpful. However, as life often goes, having a plan and executing your plan are two very different matters. Sometimes, in managing your SMART plan, you may need to make adjustments and pivot. Knowing when and how to pivot is, well, pivotal.

So, how do you execute your SMART plan effectively? How do you know when everything is going as planned? How do you know when your SMART plan isn't working, and you need to adjust it? How do you make those necessary adjustments? These are things we will cover in this chapter.

First things first: you need to commit to regular check-ins with yourself.

CHECKING IN

Goal planning is not just something you can set and forget. You have to build check-ins into your SMART plan to assess how you are progressing.

How often you check in depends on how it's going with your SMART plan. If things are going well and you're moving forward as planned, check-in every quarter of the time-bound period you've set for yourself. So, if you've selected a deadline of six months, check-in every six weeks. If the deadline is a month, check-in once a week. If you find yourself struggling regularly, you need to check in daily—identify what happened yesterday to deter you from progress so you can tweak it today.

Whether things are going well or you are struggling with your goals, tweaks will need to happen along the way.

What matters is that you commit yourself to checking in, regardless of the frequency. You owe it to yourself to honor the goal you've made an effort to achieve.

Checking in can look as simple as asking yourself: Am I hitting my target(s) and achieving the goal(s) at the specific time-bound dates I've set for myself?

One of the most valuable resources you can have in the process of checking in and changing your habits is an accountability partner.

WHEN TO HAVE AN ACCOUNTABILITY PARTNER

You might be wondering: what exactly is an accountability partner, and what does that role involve? An accountability partner is someone who helps us stick to our SMART plan and our vision. They help prevent us from allowing that resistant voice in our heads from talking ourselves out of the intentional changes we want to make, but they also serve as a cheerleader. Ultimately, an accountability partner is someone who is committed to seeing us succeed by helping us stick to our plan.

An accountability partner helps force you to rethink how you need to move forward. For example, it's easy to say you want to lose weight and get in better shape. It's easy to say you're going to go to the gym every week, Monday thru Friday at 5:00 AM. It's also easy to be awakened by your alarm clock at 4:30 AM, decide you don't feel like going, and hit the snooze button to get some more sleep. An accountability partner helps you think through your choices. Because you have to contact that person, you're forced to have a deeper discussion around your intentions to follow through (or not).

Accountability partners serve as a guide through your SMART plan. Not only can an accountability partner help hold you to the commitments to yourself, but they can also help identify weaknesses. They can help you make plans to overcome those weaknesses. Most importantly, they can help you stay on track (or get back on track) when your feelings start to overrule your rationale.

When I started my healing journey, I felt like I didn't need an accountability partner. The primary reason for this was that it seemed like no one in my life understood what I was going through with my mother. I couldn't seem to find anyone who could see past the mother/daughter relationship to the festering toxicity of it all. It can be difficult, especially when it comes to family, for people to understand how damaging some close relationships can be, particularly when they have never experienced a toxic relationship with a close family member. Even my trusted cousin would tell me, "She's still your mom, Melissa. Just give her a hug and a kiss, say 'I love you,' and walk away." That just didn't work for me. Not having anyone who genuinely understood what I was dealing with made me feel like I was on my own in my healing journey.

I did manage to heal, but looking back, I wish I would have taken more time to seek out an accountability partner that didn't use "she's still your mom" as a reason for tolerating toxic behavior. Within the past few years, I found an accountability partner that understands this dynamic. If I could have found an accountability partner like this back when I started my healing journey, it wouldn't have taken me so long to reach the point that I'm at with my mother now.

So don't give up on finding an accountability partner who wholeheartedly understands what you're going through. They could be the catalyst for significant change in your life.

The challenge lies in finding an accountability partner who wants to help you change within the context of your shared values, rather than wanting to change you to fit within what they perceive to be their values.

CHOOSING AN ACCOUNTABILITY PARTNER

So, who is a good accountability partner? The best partner to hold you accountable isn't necessarily the person closest to you. Someone who is not good at being accountable themselves is not a good candidate either. An ideal accountability partner is both an excellent critical thinker and emotionally intelligent. A critical thinker will understand your SMART plan and what it will take to achieve your goal practically. An emotionally intelligent person can handle interpersonal relationships judiciously and empathetically. That combination of traits makes for an ideal accountability partner.

"Then you will know the truth, and the truth will set you free." (John 8:28 New International Version)

"YES PEOPLE" ARE NOT GOOD ACCOUNTABILITY PARTNERS

Someone who always says "yes" to you—someone constantly looking to affirm and hype you up—will not help you stay accountable. A person might be emotionally intelligent, they might even think they want the best for you, but they lack the rationale and discipline to tell you when you're falling off your plan. They are great cheerleaders, but they lack the critical thinking or the ability to shoot you straight.

When it comes to success with your SMART goals, you need an accountability partner who will be 100% honest with you. But you, in turn, need to be committed to being open, coachable, and teachable—or else the accountability that your partner is serving up will not help you grow. At the end of this chapter, we'll review some questions to help lead you to a good accountability partner.

Many of my friends come to me for advice, and I sometimes find my emotions creeping into the advice I offer them. I'm not the best accountability partner for many of my friends due to the tight emotional connection. Friends may not be the best accountability partners for you either. When we're closely connected to someone, our feelings can often get involved. An effective accountability partner needs to manage those emotions and be consistent with their follow-through with you. If you don't have a scheduled plan for connecting for a check-in, that won't be helpful.

HOW OFTEN TO CHECK-IN WITH YOUR ACCOUNTABILITY PARTNER

How badly are you in need of accountability? The frequency in which you check in with your accountability partner depends on the gravity of the issue you're trying to overcome. Think about it this way: if you have bad chest pains, you might make an appointment with the doctor for tomorrow, but if you have *horrible* chest pains, you more than likely will go to the emergency room. Regardless of the amount of help you need sticking to your SMART plan, you need to prioritize regular sessions with your accountability partner and commit to communicating. As time goes on and you find yourself more reliably and independently following your SMART plan, you may find that you don't need to check in with them as often.

WHY YOU SHOULD STICK TO HAVING ONE ACCOUNTABILITY PARTNER

While having a support network involving multiple people you can trust is invaluable to your growth and success, working with just one accountability partner is wise. An essential facet of accountability is consistency. Suppose you're communicating with more than one accountability partner. In that case, they could tell you different things at different times, which could likely inhibit your progress with your SMART goals. It's like having too many cooks in the kitchen. It can be overwhelming and confusing, especially if you're taking direction from more than one cook on how to prep something.

However, if you choose to have more than one accountability partner, they need to work together. Both parties need to coordinate their efforts to ensure they're receiving the same information from you and are united in their approach to holding you accountable. Above all, be sure to stick with the same accountability partner(s)—not bounce around to different partners—to ensure the best results.

WHEN SOMEONE ASKS ME TO BE THEIR ACCOUNTABILITY PARTNER

When someone requests me as their accountability partner, the first thing I ask about is the outcome they're hoping to have. Once I understand their goal, I tell them what it will take to get there. This revelation often results in a change in their facial expression and tone of voice. Pursuing these healing goals is often easier said than done and involves more effort than people realize.

I have a friend who has prideful tendencies—she's a know-it-all type. She reached out to me for help with her financial struggles. She loved when I was her cheerleader, but she did not love when I challenged her to make difficult decisions. She made up excuses for why she couldn't be held accountable, and ultimately, she didn't want to do what was necessary to get herself out of her struggles. People with that personality type can be challenging to work with as an accountability partner because they are not teachable nor want to be held accountable. There's a lot of benefit in learning how to be teachable—or at least vulnerable to accountability.

As a parent, I feel being an accountable partner to my children is one of my most important jobs. If you're a parent, you likely feel the same. I want my children to be prepared for the world, and it's far better for someone who cares for them to keep it real rather than for them to get a much more painful reality check from someone who doesn't have their best interest at heart. As a banker, I'm particularly invested (pun intended) in my kids being smart with their money, so I encourage them to use a budget spreadsheet to help them stay accountable to their monthly income.

Everybody wants a good accountability partner, but many people don't want the characteristics of a good one.

James 1:8 (King James Version) says, "A double-minded man is unstable in all his ways."

KNOWING WHEN & HOW TO PIVOT A SMART PLAN

At one point or another, we all will fall off course of the plans we set for ourselves—we're human, after all. But it's okay. When this happens, you just need to adjust. Falling off your SMART plan allows you to go back and check-in with yourself. You can see where you fell off and assess why it happened—which will guide the adjustments you need to make to your SMART plan to move forward and continue progressing.

But, here's the thing: you can't quit! You need to pivot instead. If you get to the point of wanting to quit, it's time to hone in on what variables are driving you toward stopping. Your main objective with any goal should be to continue moving forward—-even if you're only moving forward an inch for a day or a month, rather than a mile.

If you find that you are not on track with what you've outlined in your SMART plan, it's time to make a change to your strategy. This does not mean you should change your vision—you might just have to change the particular path to take to achieve that vision.

One of the first signs that it's time to pivot is feeling like you've hit a wall and are no longer satisfied with following your SMART plan. Stagnancy is a sign that it's time to revise your plan. The first step in tweaking the goal is understanding the roadblock you hit with your original SMART plan. The second step is to restructure that plan so you can overcome that specific roadblock this time. Always stay passionate about the goal you want to accomplish. Keep your eyes on the prize.

During my healing process, I could feel myself getting more confident in my ability to set boundaries, but I was still irked by the behaviors of certain family members. So I asked myself how I could pivot to feel satisfied with the boundaries in place regarding my mother. For me, the answer was my garage door opener. Because she had a garage door opener, my mother had access to come into my home whenever she wanted, and she often came unannounced. By pivoting my boundary-setting goal with my mother to pursue getting my garage door opener back from her, she could no longer pop up at my home for surprise visits and invade my privacy. I set a physical boundary which served my greater goal of setting healthy boundaries with her.

It's okay to pivot as many times as necessary until you're satisfied.

Your healing process will involve a lot of unlearning and reprogramming. It's going to be tough. That's why you have to plan but also be willing to make pivots.

"*Hoping for the best, prepared for the worst, and unsurprised by anything in between.*" –Maya Angelou, *"I Know Why the Caged Bird Sings"*

Pivoting your strategy in your SMART plan doesn't just mean changing your actions—it also means making pivots in your beliefs and values. Being raised by a very religious mother who felt like I wasn't honoring her when I didn't do what she wanted,

I had to change my beliefs about what she convinced me honor meant.

Part of the difficulty in pivoting requires you to take the emotions out of intense decision-making. It can be uncomfortable. But ask yourself what you can learn from this misstep. Every pivot should be a conscious and proactive strategy to meet your goal.

OVERCOMING MY STRUGGLES WITH SMART PLANS

Over the years, I've had multiple conversations with my mother about needing to love her from a distance. The emotional and mental abuse had taken its toll on me. At a certain point in my healing journey, I made it a goal to set boundaries around my mother's communication with me. For many years, she would send me texts anyway. After asking her to stop texting me, she used Biblical scriptures to manipulate me out of those boundaries.

She would say things like, "Does God love us from a distance?"

I sent her a text in response to that question citing scriptures full of teachings that give us blueprints for how we should conduct ourselves:

"But the fruit of the Spirit is love, joy, peace, forbearance, kindness, goodness, faithfulness, gentleness and self-control.

Against such things there is no law." (Galatians 5:22–23 New International Version)

Eventually, she stopped texting me and started mailing me typed and laminated Bible content about how to treat your mother.

I needed to pivot my SMART goal to get a healthy outlet for my frustration. It tested my perseverance. I realized that I struggled the most when I didn't spend enough time in devotion or praying. Anytime I didn't do it, and I'd hear from my mother, it was like war. So I committed to getting up and doing my devotion early each morning.

It might work for you, too, if you're facing stressors through your healing journey. The key is to find a healthy outlet to keep you focused on the plan you've set forth.

APPLYING THESE LESSONS TO YOUR HEALING JOURNEY

Checking In With Yourself

1. Am I on track to meeting my goal by the deadline I've set?

_____

_____

2. Is my goal specific enough? If not, what can I change to make it more straightforward?

_____

_____

3. Do I have the right resources to achieve my goal?

_____

_____

4. What do you need to tweak? Do you need to set firmer boundaries with someone? Do you need to adjust the pace of pursuing your goal? Do you need to slow down?

_____

_____

Finding the Right Accountability Partner

When considering someone as a potential accountability partner, ask these questions:

1. Will this person be both supportive and honest?
2. Will this person be compassionately honest without protecting your feelings?
3. Is this person a critical thinker?
4. Does this person share your values?
5. Do they have the time and energy to dedicate to you?

If the answer to any of these questions is "no," they are probably not a good accountability partner.

How to Work Through a Pivot

After checking in with yourself and identifying what needs to be tweaked, it's time to pivot.

What's the stressor in your life? Can you identify it?

Ex. My mother is overstepping her boundaries

_____
_____
_____
_____

When you can identify the stressors in your life, you can make the necessary adjustments to your plan to remove those stressors. How can you adjust your current goal to remove those stressors? What aspect of your SMART plan can you change? Can you change the specificity of the goal? Can you change the way you measure it? How about making it more attainable/achievable? Can you make it more relevant to your situation? Do you need a different timeline? **Which letter(s) of SMART do you need to change, and how will you change it? Is your current system of measurement working? Is it not specific enough?**

_____
_____
_____
_____

Put your edited SMART plan into action. Continue tracking your progress. If you remove or create distance from the stressor, you will often find that achieving your goal becomes much more manageable.

If you remove that stressor but still find that you're stressed, that means there's another source of stress yet to address before you're able to progress with your plan again.

A PIVOT IN ACTION

Let's say a person who drinks a lot of soda has made a SMART goal to reduce their level of drinking down to one soda per day in four months. But checking in after two months, they realize they're still drinking two sodas a day. It's time to review: What's the stressor? Is there a person or situation triggering them to have more than one soda a day? Is the stress work-related? Is it due to a strained relationship with someone? Is it due to financial stress?

Remember that each SMART goal is part of a larger whole to heal and make progress toward your comeback. So it's okay—and expected—to pivot as many times as necessary to get where you're going.

6

VISION CONTROL

"What you get by achieving your goals is not as important as what you become by achieving your goals" –Henry David Thoreau

I can remember the joy of achieving the first goal I set in my personal life—graduating from college. I was the first college graduate in my immediate family. Graduation made me feel so accomplished and affirmed. I thought, "Dang, I *am* smart. I *can* accomplish something great and add value to my life."

It motivated me to achieve more for myself. That's a feeling I want you to get too.

WHEN TO TRY ON A NEW PAIR OF GLASSES & ADJUST YOUR VISION

As I was fighting to claim my comeback, I went through many pairs of glasses. People were telling me I didn't need a new pair because I had just bought some the previous year—that I didn't have the time to get yet another eye exam, and there was no way I could even afford a fresh pair. But I wanted a clearer picture of my vision.

As a single mother of three working a full-time corporate job and part-time jobs, I just didn't always have time to sit down and spend hours reflecting and tweaking my SMART plan. As a result, many people came to me with *their* opinion on handling the situation. It's not that this advice was unsolicited—I appreciated all the help I could get at that time in my life. But the people offering advice ultimately did not share my value of setting rigid boundaries in a toxic relationship with a parent, so I became overwhelmed by the direction they were trying to take me in. This misaligned input from people who loved me and wanted the best for me discouraged me from choosing an accountability partner.

YOU DECIDE YOUR VISION

While your vision should remain constant throughout your pursuit of your goals, you learn new things about yourself, grow, and change as you progress. That growth will bring the need for adjustments in vision driven by you. It should not come from pressure from someone else. Trying on a new pair of glasses should help you see your path. So as you try on different lenses, be sure to pick the pair that best suits you and not someone else's vision.

When you are achieving goal after goal just to find yourself in a place of stagnancy, remember that you should always be moving forward. Even a little progress is still progress.

"Idle hands are the devil's workshop; idle lips are his mouthpiece." (Proverbs 16:27 TLB)

GETTING SUPPORT WITHOUT GETTING OFF TRACK

People in your life likely want to support you in pursuing your vision and through your SMART planning—and that's wonderful. Claiming your comeback isn't easy, and you can't do it alone. We were created to be social creatures who thrive on love and support. You need help to achieve what you're going after because nothing great is ever achieved alone.

"Nothing we do, however virtuous, can be accomplished alone; therefore, we are saved by love." –Reinhold Niebuhr

Your loved ones likely want the best for you. But not everyone who cares about you will always know what's best for you. Their advice may not work for you—and that's okay. We are all humans just helping other humans, and all we *really* know with certainty is the lens through which we, as individuals, see the world. When someone who cares about you is looking at your challenges through their own pair of glasses, they very well may miss things that you can see clearly. That's important to keep in mind as you seek support. Be clear about what you need from someone: **Do you want their advice, or do you just want their support?**

When my cousin advised me to "give her a hug and a kiss, tell her I love her, and just walk away" because she's "still my mother," it was likely because that advice may have helped him in the same situation—but it didn't work for me. That doesn't mean I'm less of a person than he is; it means that his advice didn't align with what I needed to heal during that season of my life. So, it made more sense for my cousin to fill a supportive role rather than an advisory role in this case.

It can be tricky to discern what advice works for you and what doesn't. You need to be open enough to listen to the opinions of those you trust. That outside perspective can be tremendously valuable on your path to progress. But you also have to know yourself well enough to know what doesn't work for you (and be okay not taking that advice).

The consequence of not being discerning is that you will either:

(1) End up trying every piece of advice given to you, which will lead to frustration and burnout, or

(2) You will try nothing at all and lose momentum towards progress.

The more honest you are with yourself, the easier it will be to determine what's best for you. Of course, we don't always know what's best for ourselves until we get results. Often the only way you can figure out what works for you is by trial and error. It's a learning process—and the learning curve is steeper if you have less experience in life. But we are ultimately the only ones who know our values and boundaries, even if we haven't learned what those are yet. It's our responsibility to find out.

WHY YOU SHOULD NOT TAKE A BREAK

Many studies and health experts nowadays say that rest is foundational to our well-being (Asp, 2015). While rest may be good for the mind and body, rest from breaking a habit can inhibit progress. Changing your mindset and habits takes consistency. You don't have to go full-throttle; any amount of progress is acceptable. Even a baby step forward is okay, as long as your focus is to continue moving forward and not fall into a place of stagnancy.

At times, it can be tempting to take a break. After all, breaking deeply ingrained habits takes work. But claiming your comeback means breaking old patterns. And breaking habits requires consistency. So don't take your foot off the gas when you get tired—just ease up on it a tad bit.

There were times when I lost focus on my goal and found myself lingering on negativity. My suggestion to you is never to lose focus. When you start to feel like giving up, reflect on why you started down this path to claim your comeback. Reflect on how much you wanted it. Visualizing your goal is a powerful tool.

A study looking at brain patterns in weightlifters discovered that the patterns activated when a weightlifter lifted hundreds of pounds were similarly activated when they only imagined lifting. Research has revealed that mental practices are almost as effective as physical practice (Ranganathan et al., 2004).

It's okay to rest your mind, but don't fully step away from the process when you do. Spend the rest visualizing the end of your goal.

ALLOWING SPACE FOR YOUR VISION TO GROW WITH YOU

With each goal you achieve, you learn something new about what works for you—and you can replicate what works again and again! You don't have to go back and recreate the wheel when you're gearing up to overcome the next challenge because you already know of a process that works for you. That's why claiming your comeback gets easier as you go.

That being said, you're never 100% finished with claiming your comeback. Growth is an ongoing, lifelong process. We should always be working to improve ourselves.

The best thing you can do to anticipate future growth is to set yourself up for success. The more efficiently you can achieve the personal goals you set for yourself, the easier it will be to grow continuously.

My vision for my relationship with my mother was to have mutual respect with healthy boundaries—particularly around communication. My vision evolved with what I needed for healing. What started with controlling my response to her turned into physical boundaries and eventually became communication boundaries.

Give yourself the space you need for your vision to change. The focus should be on what you need to heal. You will grow in ways you may not be able to envision right now, and that new version of yourself may need something different than the version of you now. Trust your own needs and what works for you. Trust the process.

APPLYING VISION CONTROL

What pair of lenses do you need to facilitate your vision?

Are you not progressing with your goal because of something within you (internally)? Or are you in a place of stagnancy because of something happening around you (externally)?

Is the obstacle internal or external? Work with your accountability partner to determine what you need to focus on.

Do you know the difference between a vision and a mission?

A vision focuses on the future and what you need to get there. Your mission is how you execute that vision in your day-to-day life, and that's where your SMART plan comes into play.

Is your mission in alignment with your vision?

How do you define support?

This is something to think about.

Support means something different for everyone. Do you want someone who gives you space to vent? Someone to lean on? Do you want advice? Do you wish to have space and privacy to journal? A combination of two or more of these support systems? That's your support system. The type of support you need can change depending on who is available and your day-to-day situation. **What support do you believe you need right now?**

_____
_____
_____
_____
_____

1. What support do you believe you will need to get through your next SMART goal?

_____
_____
_____
_____

Knowing what kind of support you may need down the road can help you better prepare the resources you may need.

Vision Control

2. Based on your SMART plan and where you would like to be in the next three to six months, what kind of support do you believe you will need then?

Keep in mind that if you've progressed enough in your SMART plan, the kind of support you need could look different than before.

_____
_____
_____
_____
_____

Remember that it's okay if you don't stay on track with your SMART plan. If the support system you use needs to be adjusted, that's okay too. You're not obligated to take advice from anyone.

3. What are some potential goals you could set for yourself later on once you've achieved the plan you're working towards now? List one to three.

_____
_____
_____
_____
_____

7

WHAT IT TAKES TO CLAIM YOUR COMEBACK

If you've made it this far in the book, you will know that claiming your comeback isn't easy, and there is no quick fix. It's a process that involves accepting brutal truths, understanding who you are, what's best for you, and being intentional about changes to pursue a better future. But how do you know when you have claimed your comeback?

HOW YOU KNOW YOU'VE CLAIMED YOUR COMEBACK

When tension and negativity begin to give way to a sense of relief, you know you have overcome and accomplished something. You feel lighter. You feel better equipped to handle what life throws at you. But it's hard to know when you have definitively "claimed" your comeback because a comeback is an ongoing process—not a destination.

Before my comeback, I had settled with enduring toxic relationships infecting me with festering negativity. But now, I can hold these conflicting truths and be at peace with them:

1. It's important to me to have healthy relationships.

2. It takes two to form a healthy relationship, and I can only control how I show up in a relationship. I am intentional about setting healthy boundaries for myself.

3. Accepting abuse did not result in healthy relationships. Abuse on any level is never acceptable from anyone, including ourselves. Abuse is not just physical—there's emotional abuse, verbal abuse, mental and psychological abuse, financial abuse, and cultural/identity abuse. I had to recognize the abuse I'd experienced and account for it in my SMART plan.

I'm in a good season of my life now. My relationships are healthy, and I've accepted the relationship I now have with my mother. I rest assured that I have done what I could to improve our relationship and have come to terms with not having the control to force her to change. That transformation was massive for me, and it was genuinely foundational for my comeback. Your comeback will be unique to you, and it will be deeply personal for you.

KEY TAKEAWAYS FOR CLAIMING YOUR COMEBACK

1. Know Yourself

Being in touch with yourself is valuable for so many reasons. It's easier to express your needs and desires, and it also makes your experience of life more prosperous and more fulfilling. But it's particularly valuable when you're trying to break old habits.

When you know yourself, you understand what works for you and what doesn't. You know your limits and boundaries, but you also understand your potential. You make better choices because you have inner guidelines and discernment to help you navigate those decisions—whether it's something big to consider, like deciding to spend the rest of your life with a partner, or something small like what kind of shoes to buy.

You refine your self-control because you understand what motivates you to resist bad habits and empowers you to develop good habits. When grounded in your values and preferences, you are more likely to resist social pressure and less likely to say "yes" when you want to say "no." You also gain a greater understanding of others, and it's easier to extend empathy and compassion to others with awareness of your flaws and struggles. I encourage you to meditate on the nine fruits of the spirit we are to live out.

"But the fruit of the Spirit is love, joy, peace, forbearance, kindness, goodness, faithfulness, gentleness, and self-control." (Galatians 5:22-23 New International Version)

The issue with claiming your comeback without knowing yourself is that inner conflict is more likely to derail your progress. You experience far less internal conflict when you align your actions with your values and honest feelings inside. If you feel concerned that you don't know yourself well enough to confidently navigate the processes outlined in this book, I encourage you to answer the questions at the end of this chapter.

2. Deal with Your Traumas & Heal

Many of us have been through tough things in life that we may not consider traumas but are, in fact, traumas. Merriam-Webster defines trauma as "a disordered psychic or behavioral state resulting from severe mental or emotional stress or physical injury."

Minimizing what happened to you or not making a conscious realization of trauma might help you cope with life but will not allow you to heal. Whatever the case may be, you have to come to terms with your baggage if you want to move forward. Burying past traumas can result in risky behavioral changes—such as dependency on drugs, alcohol, or overeating to cope—and can even lead to medical conditions like chronic inflammation, which weakens the immune system (Roberts, 2021). The effects of trauma eventually catch up to us—it's not a matter of "if," it's a matter of "when." Traumas trigger us, especially childhood traumas. Suppose a person escapes an abusive relationship and does not get the proper counseling to heal and become whole again. In that case, they can be triggered in a future relationship, even with a nonabusive partner.

Dealing with your trauma is like pulling weeds. You can pluck a weed, but it will keep coming back if you don't pull it at the root. Your trauma will do the same—unless you address the root cause. No amount of coping you do on the surface will eradicate that trauma. You have to get down to the roots.

By now, I'm sure you can understand that my mother has experienced many traumas in her life, and these traumas ultimately affected how she treated me. My constant prayer for her is that she will desire to heal and be set free so that she can be that all God created her to be.

Do not put a mask over your traumas. That's like putting a bandaid over a wound after stepping on a grenade. Learn from the lessons life teaches you: face your traumas and heal from them rather than hiding from them. You never lose in life if you learn to become a better person through the many challenging circumstances thrown your way. Whether you were a child, a teenager, or an adult, you have to go back to that stage in your life where you experienced your trauma and dig into what it was. It will be painful work. It's difficult, time-consuming, and can be exhausting. Often, this requires the professional support of a therapist or counselor. Google "therapists near me" or "telehealth therapists" and start searching for a good match.

Note: Finding good professional support can be a process. Your first counselor might not be the right fit for you. Sometimes you have to try different counselors. Stay open to finding a good fit.

"For you formed my inward parts; you knitted me together in my mother's womb." (Psalm 139:13 English Standard Version)

God created us and knew us when we were in our mother's womb. But when we're born into this world, the world can form us—if we allow it. The world and those we are surrounded by can mold us into who we become, and that's scary. We have to keep in the forefront of our minds that we came into this world fearfully and wonderfully made, and it's up to us not to let the world convince us otherwise.

3. Aim to Thrive, Not Just Survive

When you're struggling, your mind becomes focused on simply surviving. You just want to be able to make it from one day to the next. It's a very human response to adversity, and this mindset allows us to make it through the most challenging times we experience in life. But that survival mindset should be a means to an end—it should be a temporary state of being while on your way to building the stable foundations you need to thrive. When you've healed from your traumas—or you've at least made significant progress in your healing—it's time to aim for prosperity.

When you leave this earth, that dash between your birth date and death date needs to have meant something. We're more than just beings trying to make it through life. We all have a purpose.

You can start now—it doesn't matter how old you are! You have the power to change your life no matter how you were raised or what you've had to endure. You can claim your comeback.

The key is intentionality.

It's easy to make harmful changes in your life because they lack intention. They are pleasurable, haphazard actions that release endorphins and lead to formed habits. Positive change requires intentionality, effort, and grit.

When you want to make a change as bad as you want to breathe, that's when you decide to change and commit to that intentionality. I once said out loud, "I would rather die and be at peace than live the way I'm living," and that's when I realized that I had no choice but to change for the better. You may never reach a tipping point that dire. Still, some people will, and that's accompanied by the realization that putting the work into claiming your comeback is more manageable than continuing down the same harmful path.

WHAT IT TAKES TO DO THE WORK

When unhappy people ask me for life advice, I ask them what they want out of life. The response will typically roll quickly off their tongue—that's the easy part. The hard part is taking action. That requires putting in work, and it is not often work that people want to do.

As a mother myself, I have made it a priority to put in the work to heal, to be delivered from the traumas that held me bound, to be set free, to go beyond surviving to thriving. My mother would occasionally reach out to me over the years and state she wanted a healthy relationship with me, but she was either unwilling to put the work in or just didn't know how to do it. When I didn't know how to begin my healing process, I sought a professional counselor to help me.

It's imperative, to be honest with yourself about what you can do and be humble enough to ask for help when you need it. But you also have to ask the right person. Sometimes your spouse, friend, or family member can be the right person, but sometimes you need more sound advice for getting the help you need, and a professional counselor is necessary.

Many people look at my results from CrossFit and tell me they want to work out with me. It's easy enough to say that you want to get in shape and be fit, but as you surely know, the hard part is getting to the gym and putting in the work. Even more challenging is that you may not get the same results if you put in the same effort. No two people are the same, and what works for me just may not work for you. That's a harsh truth to come to terms with, but you need to keep that in mind when you're seeking support from someone else.

IT'S ALL ABOUT THE DASH

If you plan to be buried after you have passed away (hopefully after a long life), you will have a tombstone. That tombstone will have your birth year and your death year. But those numbers aren't what really matter. What matters is that "dash" between your birth and death.

You only have this one life on earth, so you'd better make it count! What do you want that dash to represent? What do you want people to remember about you once you're gone?

IF I DID IT, SO CAN YOU

I've been through my share of hardships. I know what it's like to be deeply infected by emotional, physical, verbal, and psychological abuse through a toxic relationship. I know what it's like to have someone turn their back on you while you're trying your best to repair broken relationships. I know what it's like to go through an abusive marriage. I know what it's like to be a struggling single mother.

But I also know what it's like to overcome and finally be able to breathe a sigh of relief with gained perspective from healing. I claimed my comeback, and if I can do it—so can you.

Don't settle. I settled for a while, thinking that I would always have troubling relationships with certain people in my life. I love them deeply. However, I learned that I don't have to settle for enduring toxic relationships. I'm capable of setting respectable boundaries. And so are you.

Although you're never truly done growing in life, it's essential to reflect on the growth you've accomplished.

LOOKING AHEAD

As you look ahead to envision yourself living a life where you have claimed your comeback, it's essential to ask yourself some more important life questions. It will help you keep moving forward, even long after you have accomplished the SMART goals you set out to accomplish early on in your journey.

What are you feeling ashamed of?
_____
_____
_____

What are you worried about?
_____
_____
_____

What is your inner critic telling you?
_____
_____
_____

Complete this thought: *If I wasn't afraid, I would...*
_____
_____

What do you value?
_____
_____

What are your dreams?
_____
_____
_____

There will be dark seasons, but you will eventually get there if you remain committed to your dream and keep moving forward. It could be years or even decades. But don't give up. Stay the course.

1. What will your comeback look like? What do you imagine it will feel like? How do you envision yourself after you have made a comeback?

_____
_____
_____
_____
_____
_____
_____
_____

2. Where would you like to be with your goals five years from now? Ten years?

_____
_____
_____
_____
_____
_____
_____
_____

3. What do you want that dash in between your birth year and your death year to represent?

_____
_____
_____
_____
_____
_____
_____

ABOUT THE AUTHOR

Melissa Jones, originally from East St. Louis, embodies resilience, faith, and perseverance. She often describes herself as the female version of Joseph from the Bible—having journeyed through her own "pit seasons" over the years, she has emerged triumphant in her "palace season." Her life story is a testament to the power of overcoming adversity and staying true to one's purpose, no matter the challenges.

Melissa is an international best-selling author of the acclaimed book *Claim Your Comeback*, where she shares her journey and the transformative lessons she has learned along the way. As a dynamic keynote and motivational speaker, Melissa captivates audiences with her authenticity, passion, and practical wisdom. Her mission is to empower individuals to reclaim their lives, overcome obstacles, and achieve a lifetime of success.

Melissa's inspiring journey and impactful message have been featured on major media outlets, including ABC, NBC, Fox, CBS News, NewsNet, and in publications like the *Boston Herald*. Through her words and her work, Melissa shows others that no matter how deep the pit, there is always a path to the palace. Her powerful message of hope and determination continues to inspire people around the world to rise above their circumstances and live their best lives.

You can also catch Melissa on iHeart radio across the U.S., where she encourages listeners to focus on everything God has created them to be. Her messages are a beacon of hope and a reminder of the divine potential within each person.

Beyond her professional achievements, Melissa is the proud mother of three wonderful children who each carry a powerful legacy of their own. Her eldest, Abriana, embodies resilience and leadership in everything she does. Ajay shines with creativity and is witty, using his talents to create his own path. Her youngest, Ari, demonstrates a tenacious spirit and a heart for others, always eager to make a positive impact on those around her. Melissa's greatest joy is witnessing her children grow into individuals who inspire and empower those around them, just as she strives to do every day.

BIBLIOGRAPHY

Asp, M. (2015). Rest: A Health-Related Phenomenon and Concept in Caring Science. *Sage Journals, 2.* https://doi.org/https://doi.org/10.1177/2333393615583663/.

Bansal, V. (2021, May 19). *Fixed mindset vs growth mindset: How to shift to a path of learning and growth.* TechTello. https://www.techtello.com/fixed-mindset-vs-growth-mindset/.

Birnbaum, T., & Friedman, H. H. (2014). *Gratitude and Generosity: Two Keys to Success and Happiness.* SSRN. https://doi.org/http://dx.doi.org/10.2139/ssrn.2398117/.

Chapman, J., Jamil, R. T., & Fleisher, C. (2021). *Borderline Personality Disorder. Diagnostic and Statistical Manual of Mental Disorders, 5th Edition.* https://doi.org/10.1176/appi.books.9780890425596.295735/.

Cherry, K. (2020, December 6). *What is spiritual bypassing?* Verywell Mind. Retrieved February 10, 2022, from https://www.verywellmind.com/what-is-spiritual-bypassing-5081640.

Doran, G. T. (1981, November). There's a S.M.A.R.T. way to write management's goals and objectives. *Management Review, 70*(11), 35–36.

Drucker, P. F. (2006). *The Practice of Management.* Harper Business.

Earley, J., & Weiss, B. (2013). *Freedom from Your Inner Critic: A Self-Therapy Approach.* Sounds True, Inc.

Earley, J., & Weiss, B. (2013, December 9). *The inner critic with a legacy burden.* Personal Growth Programs. https://personal-growth-programs.com/inner-critic-legacy-burden/.

Fredrickson, B. L., Tugade, M. M., Waugh, C. E., & Larkin, G. R. (2003). What good are positive emotions in crises? A prospective study of resilience and emotions following the terrorist attacks on the United States on September 11th, 2001. *Journal of Personality and Social Psychology, 84*(2), 365–76. https://doi.org/10.1037//0022-3514.84.2.365/.

Gardner, B., Lally, P., & Wardle, J. (2012). Making health habitual: the psychology of 'habit-formation' and general practice. *British Journal of General Practice*, 62(605), 664–666. https://doi.org/doi.org/10.3399/bjgp12X659466/.

Kashdan, T. B., Uswatte, G., & Julian, T. (2005). Behaviour research and therapy. *Behaviour Research and Therapy*, 44(2), 177–199. https://doi.org/10.1016/0005-7967(93)90091-8/.

Krysinska, K., Lester, D., Lyke, J., & Corveleyn, J. (2015). Trait gratitude and suicidal ideation and behavior: An exploratory study. Crisis: *The Journal of Crisis Intervention and Suicide Prevention*, 36(4), 291–296. https://doi.org/https://doi.org/10.1027/0227-5910/a000320/.

Lawson, C. A. (2004). *Understanding the borderline mother: Helping her children transcend the intense, unpredictable, and volatile relationship.* Rowman & Littlefield.

Lin, CC. (2015). The Effect of Higher-Order Gratitude on Mental Well-Being: Beyond Personality and Unifactoral Gratitude. *Current Psychology,* 36, 127–135. https://doi.org/https://doi.org/10.1007/s12144-015-9392-0/.

Makashinyi, I. (2019, January 22). *The truth behind generational curses.* The Gospel Coalition Africa. https://africa.thegospelcoalition.org/article/truth-behind-generational-curses/.

McLanahan, S. S., & Sandefur, G. D. (1996). *Growing Up with a Single Parent: What Hurts, What Helps.* Harvard University Press.

Merriam-Webster. (n.d.). Faith. In *Merriam-Webster.com dictionary.* Retrieved August 17, 2021, from https://www.merriam-webster.com/dictionary/faith.

Merriam-Webster. (n.d.). Hope. *In Merriam-Webster.com dictionary.* Retrieved August 17, 2021, from https://www.merriam-webster.com/dictionary/hope.

Merriam-Webster. (n.d.). Trauma. *In Merriam-Webster.com dictionary.* Retrieved August 17, 2021, from https://www.merriam-webster.com/dictionary/trauma.

Bibliography

Population Reference Bureau, analysis of data from the U.S. Census Bureau, Census 2000 Supplementary Survey, 2001 Supplementary Survey, 2002 through 2019 American Community Survey.

Positive Psychology Progress: Empirical Validation of Interventions. *American Psychologist*, 60(5), 410–421. https://doi.org/https://doi.org/10.1037/0003-066X.60.5.410/.

Puff, R. (2017, September 19). *Growth mindset vs. fixed mindset.* Psychology Today. https://www.psychologytoday.com/us/blog/meditation-modern-life/201709/growth-mindset-vs-fixed-mindset/.

Seligman, M. E. P., Steen, T. A., Park, N., & Peterson, C. (2005). Positive Psychology Progress: Empirical Validation of Interventions. *American Psychologist*, 60(5), 410–421. https://doi.org/https://doi.org/10.1037/0003-066X.60.5.410/.

Ranganathan, V. K., Siemionow, V., Liu, J. Z., Sahgal, V., & Yue, G. H. (2004). From mental power to muscle power—gaining strength by using the mind. *Neuropsychologia*, 42(7), 944–956. https://doi.org/10.1016/j.neuropsychologia.2003.11.018/.

Rash, J. A., Matsuba, M. K., & Prkachin, K. M. (2011). Gratitude and Well-Being: Who Benefits the Most from a Gratitude Intervention? *Applied Psychology: Health and Well-Being*, 3(3), 350–369. https://doi.org/10.1111/j.1758-0854.2011.01058.x/.

Roberts, A. (2021, February 12). *Past trauma may haunt your future health.* Harvard Health. https://www.health.harvard.edu/diseases-and-conditions/past-trauma-may-haunt-your-future-health/.

van Buel, E. M., Sigrist, H., Fikse, L., Bosker, F. J., Schoevers, R. A., Klein, H. C., Pryce, C. R., & Eisel, U. L. M. (2017). Mouse repeated electroconvulsive seizure (ECS) does not reverse social stress effects but does induce behavioral and hippocampal changes relevant to electroconvulsive therapy (ECT) side-effects in the treatment of depression. *PLOS.* https://doi.org/ https://doi.org/10.1371/journal.pone.0184603/.

Made in the USA
Middletown, DE
05 November 2024